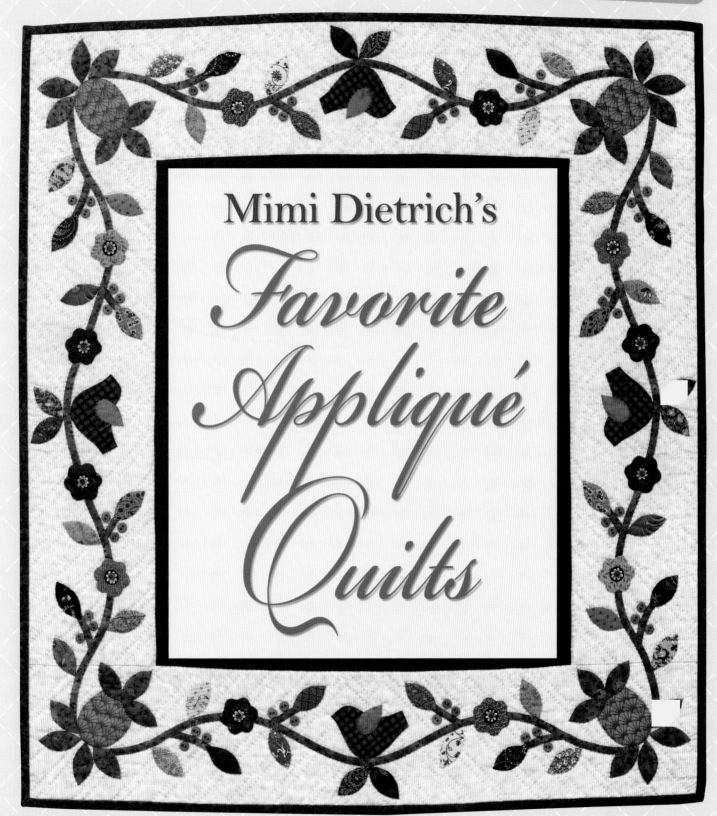

Mimi Dietrich's
Favorite Appliqué Quilts

Martingale®
& COMPANY

DEDICATION

To my students, friends, readers, and "fans"
who have stitched quilts from my books

Mimi Dietrich's Favorite Appliqué Quilts
© 2007 by Mimi Dietrich

That Patchwork Place® is an
imprint of Martingale & Company®.

Martingale & Company
20205 144th Ave. NE
Woodinville, WA 98072-8478 USA
www.martingale-pub.com

Credits
President & CEO • Tom Wierzbicki
Publisher • Jane Hamada
Editorial Director • Mary V. Green
Managing Editor • Tina Cook
Developmental Editor: Karen Costello Soltys
Technical Editor • Laurie Baker
Copy Editor • Durby Peterson
Design Director • Stan Green
Assistant Design Director • Regina Girard
Illustrator • Laurel Strand
Cover Designer • Shelly Garrison
Text Designer • Regina Girard
Photographer • Brent Kane

Printed in China
12 11 10 09 08 07   8 7 6 5 4 3 2 1

Library of Congress Cataloging-in-Publication Data
Library of Congress Control Number: 2007028088

ISBN: 978-1-56477-679-2

Mission Statement
Dedicated to providing quality
products and service to inspire creativity.

Contents

Introduction 5

PROJECTS

Heirloom Hearts 6

Bright Songs 32

Angels of Comfort 64

Springtime in Baltimore 12

Anniversary Roses 40

Appliqué Sampler 72

Redwork Bouquet 22

Hope Blossoms 46

Monogram Wreath 78

Cottage Flowerpots 26

Yo-Yo Berries 50

Glorious Girl 82

Mini Mimi 58

Quiltmaking Techniques 83

Writings of Mimi Dietrich 95

About the Author 96

Introduction

This all started with a happy ending! Twenty years ago I wrote my first quilting book, *Happy Endings: Finishing the Edges of Your Quilt,* for That Patchwork Place. That year at International Quilt Market, Nancy Martin, the president of That Patchwork Place, took me aside and asked, "Well, what are you going to do next?" It had never occurred to me that I would write more than one book! But Nancy opened my mind to new possibilities and made me think. What about a book of my favorite handmade-quilt techniques? What about my favorite appliqué techniques? What about new quilts based on the antique quilts in the Smithsonian Institution collection? What about a book to celebrate being a cancer survivor? Nancy encouraged me to be myself and combine my favorite appliqué techniques with patchwork designs in quilts that are fun and easy to make.

I like to keep things simple so that almost any quilter can be successful in stitching my designs. After 30 years of quilting, I tell students that I'm at the age where I don't have to do things that are too complicated. I get inspired by traditional quilts and designs, and I choose to make quilts with easy techniques so that other quilters will also want to make them. I like to teach appliqué techniques because I enjoy helping students learn the basics and feel successful. Some students want to learn just the beginner skills, and others use these techniques to give themselves confidence to stitch more complicated designs.

Where does creativity come from? I think it comes when we least expect it, but we need to be open to new ideas. I love to relax, read, look at magazines, or take a walk on a cool day and look at the gardens in my neighborhood. You never know when you'll see a color or a shape that will inspire you to do something different. My best ideas seem to arrive when I'm just trying to relax—and then I start dreaming up new quilt designs!

What's my favorite part of the quilting experience? You guessed it—appliqué! I can't paint or draw, so I feel as though I am creating pictures with appliqué. I love to see the black-and-white drawings come to life with colorful fabrics. I love to feel the fabrics and threads in my hands. I love silver thimbles. I love to sit back in my favorite chair with my favorite light and a big glass of iced tea—and stitch!

After writing 13 quilting books, I am celebrating my career as a quilt-book writer with *Mimi Dietrich's Favorite Appliqué Quilts.* Many of these quilt designs are in books that are now out of print, and students often ask me for the patterns. (For more information about the titles mentioned in this book, and to see which ones are currently in print, refer to the bibliography on page 95.) The patterns in this book are my favorites for many reasons: students succeed when I teach these designs in my appliqué classes, the simplicity of the designs encourages quilters to make the quilts, and the projects are fun! With a little help from my friends, I've stitched some of the original designs in new colors, made them with new techniques, and laid them out in new arrangements. I've also borrowed some wonderful quilts from my students. I enjoy getting students and friends involved in my work—they inspire me!

 I hope my favorite quilts inspire you to appliqué!

Heirloom Hearts

by Mimi Dietrich and Lucy Haw, from Handmade Quilts

FINISHED QUILT: 30½" x 30½"

FINISHED BLOCK: 10" x 10"

*W*here does it come from, this passion for quilting? My great grandmother was a quilter, and I slept under one of her handmade appliquéd quilts when I was growing up. I loved the feel of the fabrics from the 1930s and spent many hours studying the design to see if any two Dresden Plate blocks were exactly the same. I even remember picking at the stitches to see how the quilt was made! My mom was not a quilter, but she loved to embroider and make things with her hands. I'm sure she taught me to love handwork just by her example. She embroidered "Heirloom Hearts" for my second book, Handmade Quilts. When she died, the thing I wanted most was her silver thimble. I treasure it, knowing how much pleasure and comfort it gave her when she used it.

MATERIALS

Yardages are based on 42"-wide fabrics.

1⅝ yards of cream fabric for block backgrounds, border, and binding

⅛ yard *each* of light pink, medium pink, light blue, medium blue, light lavender, and medium lavender fabrics for appliqué pieces

1 yard of fabric for backing

35" x 35" piece of batting

2½ yards of 1"-wide beading lace

4 yards of ¼"-wide pink ribbon

Mechanical pencil or your favorite wash-out fabric marker

Embroidery floss: light green, lavender, blue, yellow, white, and pink

Size 8 embroidery needle

Embroidery hoop

CUTTING

All measurements include ¼"-wide seam allowances.

From the cream fabric, cut:

4 squares, 10½" x 10½"*

4 strips, 5½" x 32"

4 binding strips, 2" x 42"

*If you wish, you can cut the squares 1" larger (11½" x 11½") and trim them to 10½" x 10½" after completing the appliqués and embroidery.

APPLIQUÉING AND EMBROIDERING THE BLOCKS

1. Enlarge the pattern on page 10 to 110%. Fold the cream 10½" background squares into quarters and gently crease the folds. Match the center folds of each square to the center marks on the enlarged pattern. Lightly trace the design onto each square.

2. Make a template for the appliquéd heart from the enlarged pattern. Use the template and your favorite method to cut and prepare the appliqué pieces from the appropriate appliqué fabrics, referring to the photo as necessary.

3. Appliqué the heart pieces to each background square where indicated by the traced hearts, referring to the photo on page 6 for color placement if needed.

4. Place each square in an embroidery hoop for embroidering. Using a hoop while stitching will keep your fabric flat and your stitches from puckering. Refer to "Embroidery Stitches" on page 88 to embroider the remaining marks as follows using two strands of embroidery floss. Remove the fabric from the hoop when you are not stitching.

   Stems: light green stem stitch

   Leaves: light green single lazy daisy stitch

   Small flowers: lavender lazy daisy stitch

   Larger flowers: blue lazy daisy stitch

   Flower centers: yellow French knots

   Lace: white French knots

   Small hearts: pink satin stitch

   Lace edge: white blanket stitch

MAKING THE BORDERS

1. Enlarge the border embroidery patterns on page 11 to 250%. Each of the four border patterns will require more than one piece of paper to make a complete pattern; tape the papers together for each border.

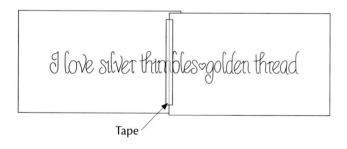

Tape

2. Center the cream 5½" x 32" strips over each of the four border patterns and trace the letters and hearts. (The corner designs will be added later.)

3. Embroider the letters using a chain stitch and two strands of blue embroidery floss. Satin stitch the small hearts using two strands of pink embroidery floss.

ASSEMBLING THE QUILT TOP

Refer to the quilt assembly diagram below, "Straight Sets" on page 89, and "Mitered Corners" on page 90 to assemble your quilt top.

1. If you cut the background squares oversized, trim them to 10½" square, being careful to center the design in each block.

2. Sew the blocks into two rows of two blocks each. I like to press the seam allowances open to distribute the seam shadows. Sew the rows together. Press the seam allowances open.

3. Sew the border strips to the quilt top, mitering the corners.

4. Trace the full-sized border corner pattern on page 9 onto each quilt corner. Appliqué the remaining heart shapes to the center of each marked design. Embroider the remaining marks to match the center of the quilt.

5. Sew the beading lace over the border seams, neatly mitering each corner. Cut the ribbon into four equal lengths. Thread a length of pink ribbon through the lace on each side of the quilt, leaving a tail at each end to tie a bow. Tie a bow at each corner.

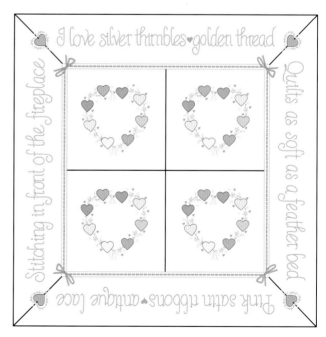

Quilt assembly

FINISHING THE QUILT

Refer to "Finishing Techniques" on page 91 as needed to complete the following steps.

1. Layer the quilt top with the batting and backing. Baste the layers together.

2. Hand or machine quilt as desired.

3. Square up the quilt sandwich.

4. Prepare and sew the cream binding strips to the quilt. Add a hanging sleeve, if desired, and a label.

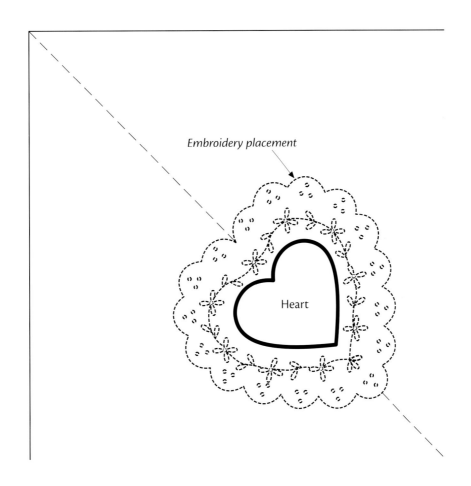

Embroidery placement

Heart

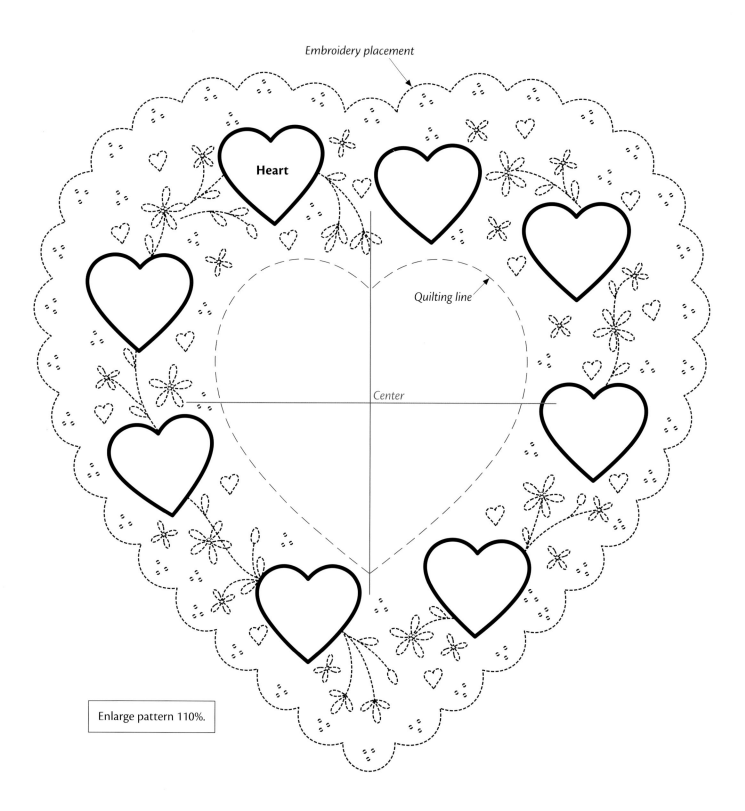

Embroidery placement

Heart

Quilting line

Center

Enlarge pattern 110%.

Enlarge patterns 250%.

I love silver thimbles♥golden thread

Top border

Quilts as soft as a feather bed

Right border

Pink satin ribbons♥antique lace

Bottom border

Stitching in front of the fireplace

Left border

Springtime in Baltimore

by Mimi Dietrich

FINISHED QUILT: 31½" x 31½"

FINISHED BLOCK: 10" x 10"

I live in Baltimore, Maryland. It has always been my home. For the last 16 years, I have taught a yearlong Baltimore Album appliqué class at my local quilt shop. I love getting to know the students throughout the year, and I feel as though we are truly recreating quilting history here in my hometown.

It has been almost 30 years since I saw my first antique Baltimore Album quilt and fell in love with the beautiful appliqué designs. Traditionally, Baltimore quilts are predominantly bright red and green, the colors I used for "Welcome to Baltimore," but it was fun to stitch the designs in pastel colors for a change. The antique quilts have inspired my own quilts, so I always feel right at home stitching appliqué designs with a needle, thread, and thimble.

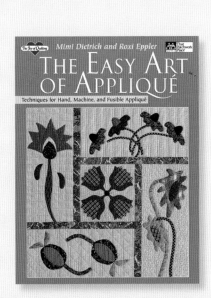

Welcome to Baltimore *from* The Easy Art of Appliqué

MATERIALS

Yardages are based on 42"-wide fabrics.

1 ⅜ yards of white-on-white print for block backgrounds and outer border

¾ yard of pink print for appliqué pieces, inner border, and binding

½ yard of medium green print for stems

¼ yard *each* of medium blue, light blue, and medium gold prints for appliqué pieces

¼ yard of light gold print for dimensional buds

1 yard of fabric for backing

35" x 35" piece of batting

Mechanical pencil or your favorite wash-out fabric marker

CUTTING

All measurements include ¼"-wide seam allowances.

From the white-on-white print, cut:

4 squares, 10½" x 10½"*

4 strips, 5½" x 33"

From the light gold print, cut:

8 squares, 1½" x 1½"

From the medium green print, cut:

1¼ yards *total* of ½"-wide bias strips

From the pink print, cut:

2 strips, 1" x 20½"

2 strips, 1" x 21½"

4 binding strips, 2" x 42"

If you wish, you can cut the squares 1" larger (11½" x 11½") and trim them to 10½" x 10½" after completing the appliqués.

APPLIQUÉING THE BLOCKS

1. Fold the white 10½" background squares into quarters and gently crease the folds. Lightly trace one of the full-sized patterns on pages 16–19 onto each square, matching the center fold of each square to the center mark of the pattern.

2. Make appliqué templates for the blocks using the patterns on pages 16–19. Cut and prepare the appliqué pieces from the appropriate appliqué fabrics using your favorite method and referring to the photo on page 12 as necessary.

3. Appliqué the pieces for each block to the background squares in numerical order using your favorite appliqué technique. Refer to "Stem Method One" on page 85 to appliqué the stems, and to "Dimensional Buds" on page 87 to fold the light gold squares into dimensional buds and appliqué them in place.

APPLIQUÉING THE BORDERS

1. Using the full-sized pattern on page 20, and referring to the quilt photo on page 12, trace a complete border design pattern onto 5½"-wide pieces of paper, taping the paper together as necessary. Center each outer-border fabric strip over the pattern and trace the swags and hearts onto the fabric. The corner flower shapes will be added after the quilt is assembled.

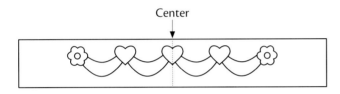

Center

2. Make appliqué templates for the border strips using your favorite method and the patterns on pages 20 and 21. Cut and prepare the appliqué pieces from the appropriate appliqué fabrics, referring to the quilt photo as necessary.

3. Appliqué the swags and then the hearts to the border strips using your favorite appliqué technique.

ASSEMBLING THE QUILT TOP

Refer to the quilt assembly diagram at right, "Straight Sets" on page 89, and "Mitered Corners" on page 90 to assemble your quilt top.

1. If you cut the background squares oversized, trim them to 10½" square, being careful to center the design in each block.

2. Sew the blocks into two rows of two blocks each. I press the seam allowances open to distribute the seam shadows. Sew the rows together. Press the seam allowances open.

3. Sew the pink 1" x 20½" inner-border strips to the sides of the quilt top. Sew the pink 1" x 21½" inner-border strips to the top and bottom of the quilt top.

4. Sew the white-on-white 5½" x 33" outer-border strips to the quilt top, mitering the corners.

5. Using the pattern on page 21, trace the corner appliqué design onto each corner of the outer border, and then appliqué the flowers, leaves, and ribbons that you made in step 2 of "Appliquéing the Borders" in place in numerical order.

Quilt assembly

FINISHING THE QUILT

Refer to "Finishing Techniques" on page 91 as needed to complete the following steps.

1. Layer the quilt top with the batting and backing. Baste the layers together.

2. Hand or machine quilt as desired.

3. Square up the quilt sandwich.

4. Prepare and sew the pink binding strips to the quilt. Add a hanging sleeve, if desired, and a label.

*Dimensional bud

Dimensional bud

Springtime in Baltimore

Center

*Dimensional bud

2

2

7

9

10

8

1

3

4*

2

2

3

4*

Center

3

4*

2

2

4*

2

8

3

5

9

7

6

2

2

*Dimensional bud

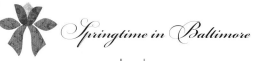
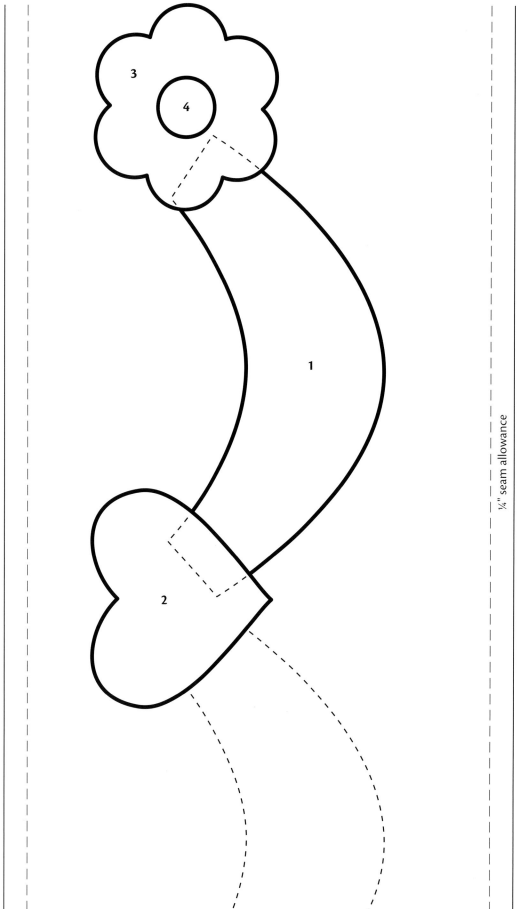

¼" seam allowance

¼" seam allowance

Redwork Bouquet

by Mimi Dietrich

FINISHED QUILT: 22¼" x 22¼"

FINISHED BLOCK: 9" x 9"

*H*ere's a chance to "stitch outside of the block." I love to encourage students to take appliqué patterns and change them to add personal touches to their quilts. The refrain "It's your quilt, you can do anything!" is often heard in my classes. Did you know that you can use appliqué patterns for other quilting techniques? My friends Karan Flanscha and Libbie Rollman like to embroider blocks with redwork designs. They simply trace appliqué designs and embroider the lines with stem stitches and French knots. This opens their world to a new collection of designs and adds an entirely new look to an old favorite. The inspiration for "Redwork Bouquet" was a quilt featured on the cover of Baltimore Bouquets.

Flower Bouquet, *cover quilt from* Baltimore Bouquets

MATERIALS

Yardages are based on 42"-wide fabrics.

⅞ yard of red floral for setting triangles and outer border

⅜ yard of white-on-white print for embroidery-block background

⅓ yard of black print for inner border and binding

⅞ yard of fabric for backing

26" x 26" piece of batting

Mechanical pencil or fine-tipped permanent red marker

2 skeins of red embroidery floss (I used a variegated floss, Anchor 1206)

Size 8 embroidery needle

Embroidery hoop

CUTTING

All measurements include ¼"-wide seam allowances.

From the white-on-white print, cut:

1 square, 9½" x 9½"*

From the red floral, cut:

2 squares, 7¼" x 7¼"; cut once diagonally to yield 4 triangles

2 strips, 4" x 15¼"

2 strips, 4" x 22¼"

From the black print, cut:

2 strips, 1½" x 13¼"

2 strips, 1½" x 15¼"

3 binding strips, 2" x 42"

*If you wish, you can cut the square 1" larger (10½" x 10½") and trim it to 9½" x 9½" after completing the embroidery.

EMBROIDERING THE BLOCK

1. Fold the white 9½" square *diagonally* into quarters and gently crease the folds. Match the center folds to the center marks on the full-sized pattern on page 25. Lightly trace the design onto the square.

2. Place the marked square in an embroidery hoop. Using a hoop while stitching will keep your fabric flat and your stitches from puckering. Refer to "Embroidery Stitches" on page 88 to use a stem stitch and two strands of red embroidery floss to embroider the lines. Use a French knot and three strands of red embroidery floss for the dots. Remove the fabric from the hoop when you are not stitching.

Twice as Nice

You can embroider and quilt at the same time, and be assured that any red thread "tails" will not shadow through the background fabric! This is Karan Flanscha's signature technique. After marking the design on the background square, assemble the quilt top. Baste the quilt top to thin cotton batting and then embroider through both layers. When the embroidery is finished, add the quilt back and quilt the setting triangles and borders. You will love the way the "quilted embroidery" looks.

ASSEMBLING THE QUILT TOP

Refer to the photo on page 22 and "Overlapped Corners" on page 89 to assemble your quilt top.

1. If you cut the background square oversized, trim it to 9½" square, being careful to center the design in the block.

2. Sew red floral triangles to opposite sides of the embroidered square. Press the seam allowances toward the triangles. Repeat on the remaining sides of the square.

3. Sew the black 1½" x 13¼" inner-border strips to the sides of the quilt top. Sew the black 1½" x 15¼" inner-border strips to the top and bottom of the quilt top.

4. Sew the red 4" x 15¼" outer-border strips to the sides of the quilt top. Sew the red 4" x 22¼" outer-border strips to the top and bottom of the quilt top.

FINISHING THE QUILT

Refer to "Finishing Techniques" on page 91 as needed to complete the following steps.

1. Layer the quilt top with the batting and backing. Baste the layers together.

2. Hand or machine quilt as desired.

3. Square up the quilt sandwich.

4. Prepare and sew the black binding strips to the quilt. Add a hanging sleeve, if desired, and a label.

Center

Cottage Flowerpots

by Mimi Dietrich, machine quilted by Linda Newsom

FINISHED QUILT: 52" x 60½"

FINISHED BLOCK: 8½" x 8½"

I love flowers! However, I'm not a very good gardener—it's something about the dirt—so I like to appliqué flowers on many of my quilts. The nice thing about appliquéd flowers is that they bloom all year. A floral quilt reminds me of the beauty of nature, even in the coldest weather.

Some of my favorite designs have blossomed in appliquéd flowerpots—tulips, heart flowers, and dimensional violets—throughout many of my books. This little quilt is a sampler of flowers I love.

I also enjoy fabric collections (don't we all!). I bought the fabrics for this quilt from a vendor at a quilt show. The fat quarters were tied together with a pretty bow, and I just couldn't resist them. I knew I would use the collection for a special project, and here it is.

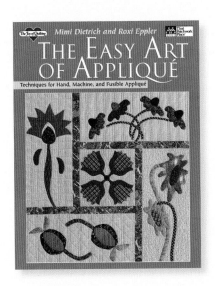

Miniature Violets
from The Easy
Art of Appliqué

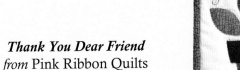

Thank You Dear Friend
from Pink Ribbon Quilts

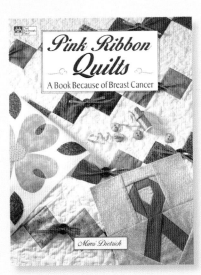

MATERIALS

Yardages are based on 42"-wide fabrics.

2⅝ yards of blue floral for outer border and binding

1¼ yards *total* of assorted medium tan prints for block corners

⅞ yard of light tan print for block backgrounds

⅜ yard of red print for appliqué pieces and inner border

Scraps of assorted red, pink, blue, and green prints for flowers and leaves

Scraps of assorted dark tan prints for flowerpots

3¼ yards of fabric for backing

56" x 65" piece of batting

Mechanical pencil or your favorite wash-out fabric marker

CUTTING

All measurements include ¼"-wide seam allowances.

From the light tan print, cut:

4 strips, 6½" x 42"; crosscut into 20 squares, 6½" x 6½"*

From the assorted medium tan prints, cut a *total* of:

40 squares, 5⅛" x 5⅛"; cut once diagonally to yield 80 triangles

From the red print, cut:

2 strips, 1¾" x 34½"

3 strips, 1¾" x 42"

From the blue floral, cut:

2 strips, 8" x 37", along the *lengthwise* grain

2 strips, 8" x 60½", along the *lengthwise* grain

7 yards *total* of 2¼"-wide bias binding strips

*If you wish, you can cut the strips 1" wider and the squares 1" larger (7½" x 7½") and trim the squares to 6½" x 6½" after completing the appliqués.

APPLIQUÉING THE SQUARES

1. Fold the light tan 6½" squares *diagonally* into quarters and gently crease the folds. Match the center folds to the center marks on the full-sized main pattern on page 31. Begin by tracing the flowerpot and leaf appliqué designs onto each square. Then trace the tulip design onto four squares. Using the patterns on page 30, trace the heart design onto nine squares, and the circle flower design onto four squares. Mark the placement for the gathered flowers onto the remaining three squares.

2. Make appliqué templates using the patterns on pages 30 and 31. Cut and prepare the appliqué pieces from the appropriate appliqué fabrics using your favorite method and referring to the photo on page 26 as necessary. Cut 1½" squares from the desired fabrics for the tulip centers. Cut 3" circles for the gathered blossoms (template on page 87).

3. Appliqué the pieces for each block to the background squares in numerical order using your favorite appliqué technique. Do not turn under the top edge of the flowerpot base. You will cover it with the flowerpot rim. Refer to "Dimensional Buds" on page 87 to make the centers of the tulips from the 1½" squares, "Perfect Circles" on page 86 to make the circle flowers, and "Gathered Blossoms" on page 87 to make the nine gathered flowers from the 3" circles.

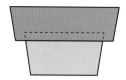

MAKING THE BLOCKS

1. If you cut the appliquéd squares oversized, trim them to 6½" square, being careful to center the design in each block.

2. Sew medium tan print triangles to opposite sides of each appliquéd square. Press the seam allowances toward the triangles. Repeat on the remaining sides of each square to complete the blocks.

ASSEMBLING THE QUILT TOP

Refer to the quilt assembly diagram below, "Straight Sets" on page 89, and "Overlapped Corners" on page 89 to assemble your quilt top.

1. Arrange the blocks into five rows of four blocks each as shown or as desired. Sew the blocks together in each row. Press the seam allowances in opposite directions from row to row. Sew the rows together. Press the seam allowances in one direction.

2. Sew the red 1¾" x 34½" inner-border strips to the top and bottom of the quilt top. Sew the three red 1¾" x 42" inner-border strips together end to end to make one long strip. From the pieced strip, cut two strips, 1¾" x 45½". Sew these strips to the sides of the quilt top.

3. Sew the blue 8" x 37" outer-border strips to the top and bottom of the quilt top. Sew the blue 8" x 60½" outer-border strips to the sides of the quilt top.

Quilt assembly

4. To mark the scalloped edge, use the fabric marker to mark a dot 1½" from the raw edges of the quilt, directly across from the corners of each block as shown. Draw a curve from dot to dot that touches the outer edge of the quilt at the curve's outermost point. Round off the corners of the quilt. Do not trim the curves until you have applied the binding.

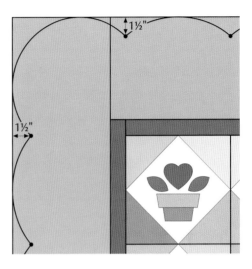

FINISHING THE QUILT

Refer to "Finishing Techniques" on page 91 as needed to complete the following steps.

1. Layer the quilt top with the batting and backing. Baste the layers together.

2. Hand or machine quilt as desired.

3. Square up the quilt sandwich.

4. Prepare and sew the blue bias binding strips to the quilt. Ease the binding along the outer edge of each curve. At each inner point, leave the needle in the fabric, pivot, turn the binding to match the next curve, and continue sewing the next curve. Trim the edge of the quilt even with the binding when you are finished sewing it in place. Turn the binding to the back of the quilt and stitch it in place, folding a miter in the binding at each inner point.

5. Add a hanging sleeve, if desired, and a label.

Dutch Treat *from* Basic Quiltmaking
Techniques for Hand Appliqué

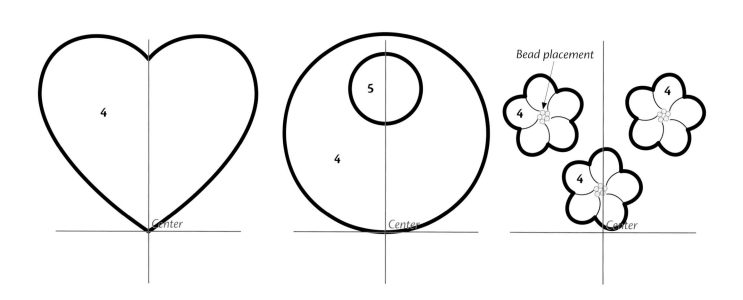

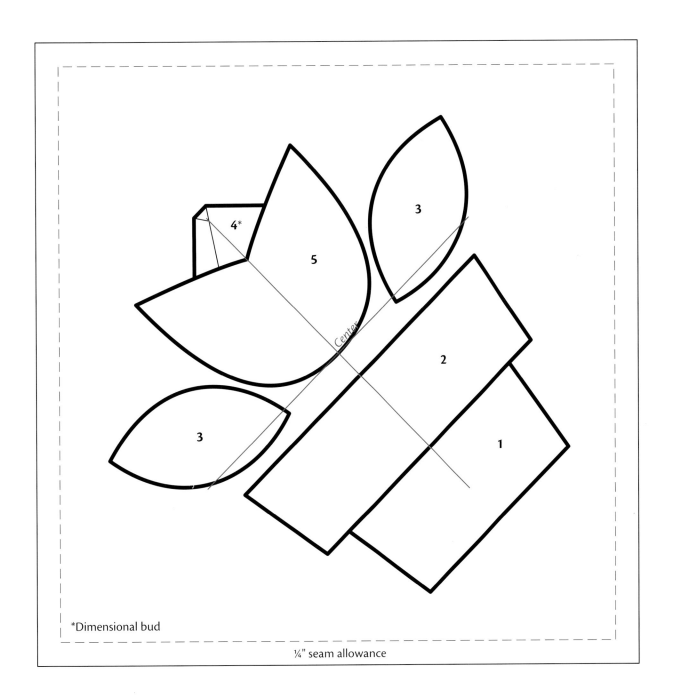

4*

5

3

Center

2

3

1

*Dimensional bud

¼" seam allowance

Bright Songs

by Mimi Dietrich,
machine quilted by Linda Newsom

FINISHED QUILT: 18" x 43½"

FINISHED BLOCK: 6" x 6"

*N*ature is a wonderful inspiration for appliqué. Take a walk outside and notice the world around you. The seasons provide a collection of beautiful themes that can be interpreted in quilts—spring flowers, summer sunshine, autumn colors, and sparkling snowflakes. Take a small child along on a walk, and through a child's eyes you will see things you didn't notice before. My two-year-old granddaughter, Julia, stopped during a walk and pointed up, saying "Bird!" and inviting me to listen a little closer to the world. As you shop for fabrics, it's fun to find some that reflect the colors and feelings of the scenery in your environment.

The appliqués for this quilt were originally cut from more subdued fabrics and arranged in a square setting, but these birds will sing for you no matter how you color or place them.

Songs for All Seasons *from* Basic Quiltmaking Techniques for Hand Appliqué

MATERIALS

Yardages are based on 42"-wide fabrics.

⅔ yard of multicolored batik print for outer border and binding

⅜ yard of medium green batik print for setting triangles and stems

¼ yard of light yellow print for block backgrounds

¼ yard of bright pink print for inner border

⅛ yard of bright yellow print for bird, flower, and leaf

⅛ yard of orange batik for bird, flower center, and leaf

⅛ yard of bright blue batik for bird

⅛ yard of purple batik for bird

⅛ yard of red batik for bird and cherries

⅛ yard of dark green batik print for leaves

Scrap of black fabric for red bird's beak

1½ yards of fabric for backing

22" x 48" piece of batting

Mechanical pencil or your favorite wash-out fabric marker

Green embroidery floss

Size 8 embroidery needle

Buttons: 4 small white for eyes; 1 medium red for holly berry

CUTTING

All measurements include ¼"-wide seam allowances.

From the light yellow print, cut:

4 squares, 6½" x 6½"*

From the multicolored batik print, cut:

2 strips, 4" x 36½"

2 strips, 4" x 18"

4 binding strips, 2" x 42"

From the medium green batik print, cut:

2 squares, 9¾" x 9¾"; cut twice diagonally to yield 8 triangles (there will be 2 extra)

2 squares, 5¼" x 5¼"; cut once diagonally to yield 4 triangles

4 bias strips, ½" x 9"

From the bright pink print, cut:

2 strips, 1½" x 34½"

2 strips, 1½" x 11"

*If you wish, you can cut the squares 1" larger (7½" x 7½") and trim them to 6½" x 6½" after completing the appliqués.

APPLIQUÉING THE BLOCKS

1. Fold the 6½" background squares *diagonally* into quarters and gently crease the folds. Lightly trace one of the full-sized patterns on page 36–39 onto each square, matching the center fold of each square to the center mark on the pattern.

2. Make appliqué templates for the blocks using the patterns on pages 36–39. Cut and prepare the appliqué pieces from the appropriate appliqué fabrics using your favorite method and referring to the photo on page 32 as necessary. If you use the freezer-paper appliqué method described on page 83, trace the bird bodies and the red bird's beak in reverse.

3. Appliqué the pieces for each block to the background squares in numerical order using your favorite appliqué technique. Refer to "Stem Method One" on page 85 to appliqué the stems and to "Perfect Circles" on page 86 to appliqué the circles. If you are using the freezer-paper method, remove the freezer paper behind the bird bodies before appliquéing the wings.

4. Refer to "Embroidery Stitches" on page 88 to stem stitch the cherry stems using two strands of green embroidery floss.

5. On each block, sew a small white button where indicated for the bird's eye. Sew the red button below the red bird.

ASSEMBLING THE QUILT TOP

Refer to the quilt assembly diagram at right, "Diagonal Sets" on page 89, and "Overlapped Corners" on page 89 to assemble your quilt top.

1. If you cut the background squares oversized, trim them to 6½" square, being careful to center the design in each block.

2. Arrange the appliquéd blocks and setting triangles as shown. Sew the blocks and triangles together to form diagonal rows. Press the seam allowances toward the setting triangles. Join the rows, adding the corner setting triangles last. Press the seam allowances in one direction.

3. Sew the pink 1½" x 34½" inner-border strips to the sides of the quilt top. Sew the pink 1½" x 11" inner-border strips to the top and bottom of the quilt top.

4. Sew the multicolored batik 4" x 36½" outer-border strips to the sides of the quilt top. Sew the multicolored batik 4" x 18" outer-border strips to the top and bottom of the quilt top.

Quilt assembly

FINISHING THE QUILT

Refer to "Finishing Techniques" on page 91 as needed to complete the following steps.

1. Layer the quilt top with the batting and backing. Baste the layers together.

2. Hand or machine quilt as desired.

3. Square up the quilt sandwich.

4. Prepare and sew the multicolored batik binding strips to the quilt. Add a hanging sleeve, if desired, and a label.

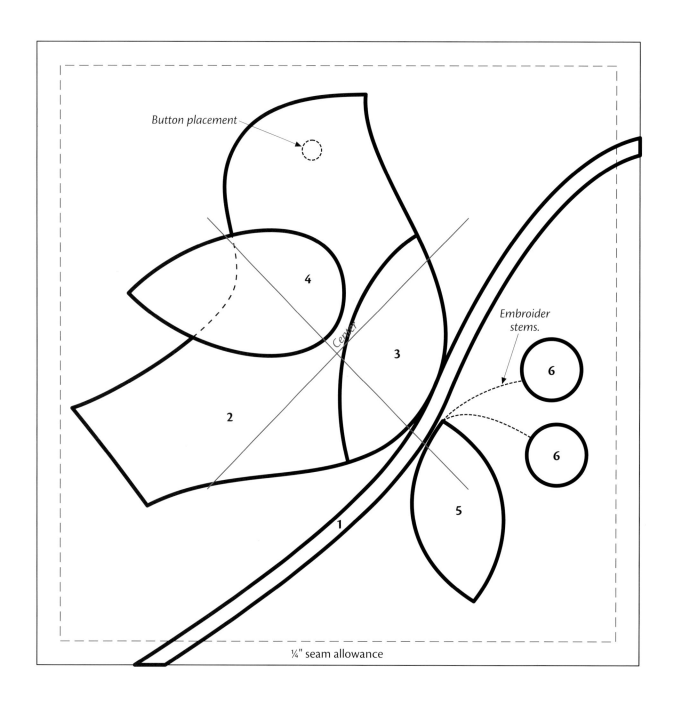

Button placement

Embroider
stems.

Center

4

3

2

5

1

6

6

¼" seam allowance

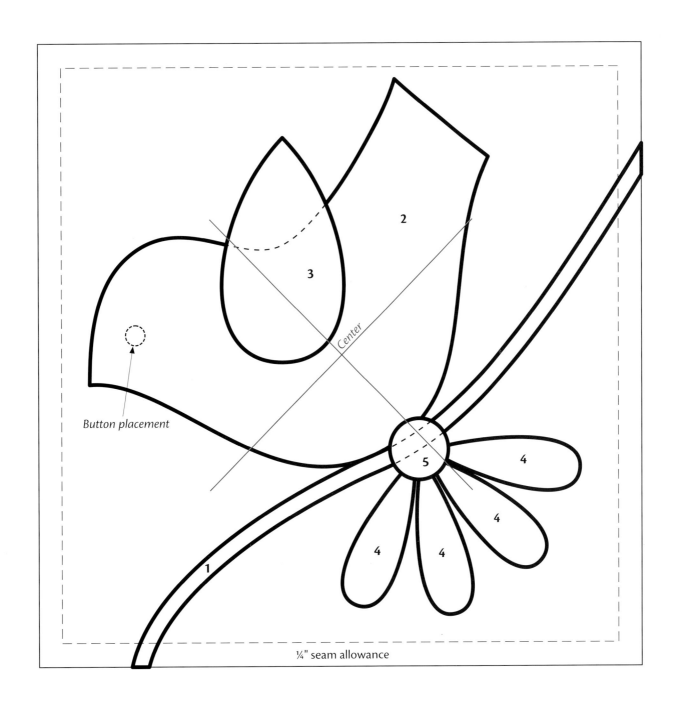

Button placement

Center

¼" seam allowance

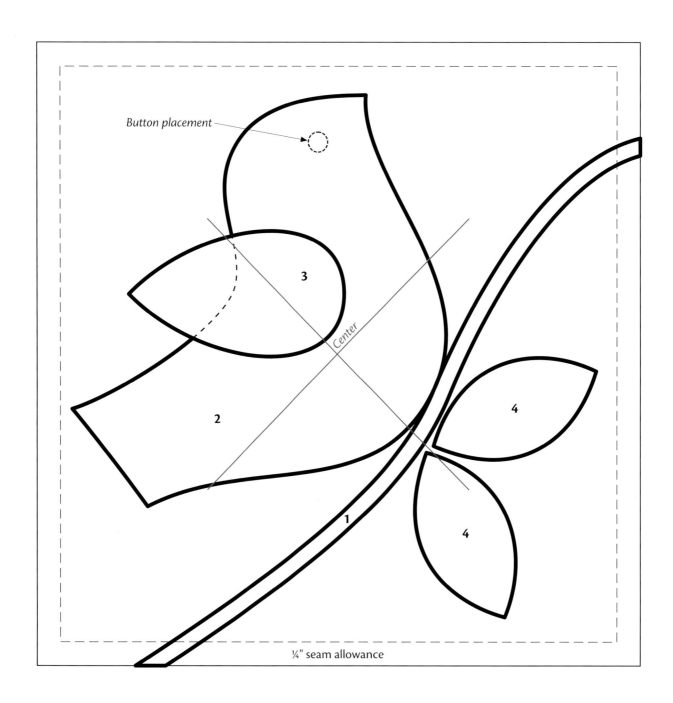

Button placement

3

2

Center

4

4

1

¼" seam allowance

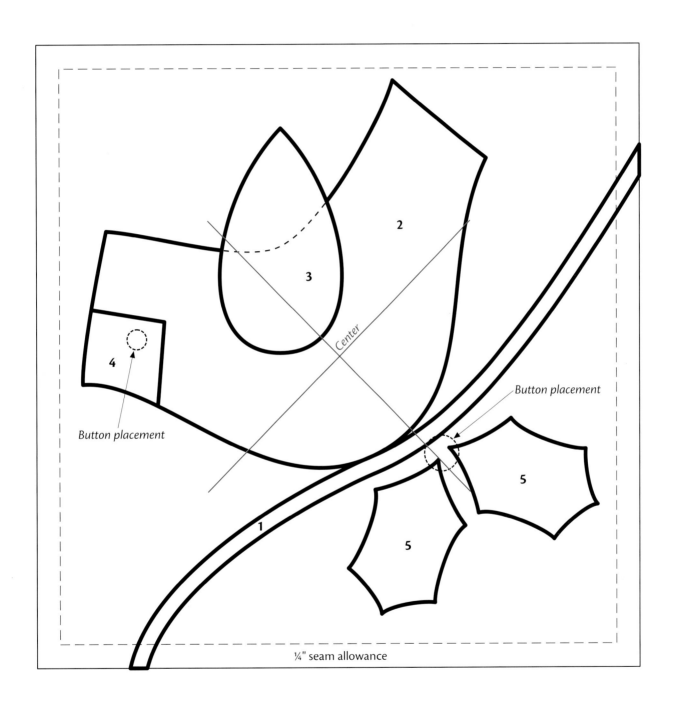

2

3

4

Button placement

Center

Button placement

5

1

5

¼" seam allowance

Anniversary Roses

by Sharon Adams

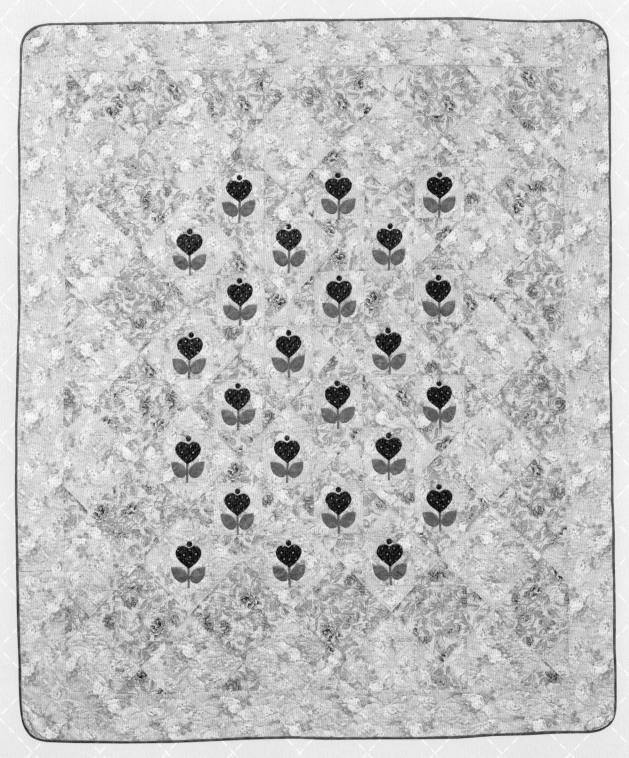

FINISHED QUILT: 71½" x 83½"

FINISHED BLOCK: 6" x 6"

*Y*es, I love hearts! They make me happy; they make me think about love. Obviously, my friend Sharon Adams, who made this quilt for her wedding anniversary, loves them as well.

One of my favorite sayings is "Do what you love; love what you do." And I do love what I do! I play with fabric, create quilt designs, write quilting books, and teach appliqué classes to quilters, the best group of people in the world. I've used the heart shape in many of my quilts, and I like to use it to teach basic appliqué to students because the shape is made of straight lines, curved lines, and inside and outside points. If you can learn to appliqué a heart, that can give you confidence to appliqué other pieces.

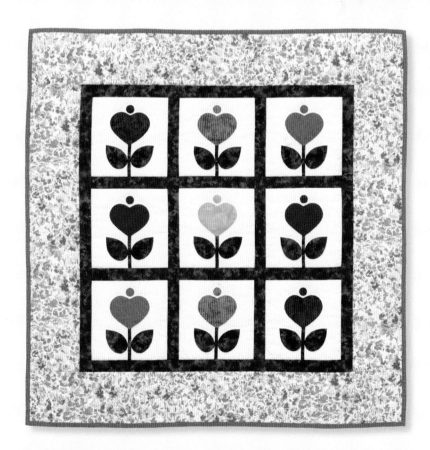

Rainbow Roses *from* Basic Quiltmaking Techniques for Hand Appliqué

 *Anniversary Roses*

MATERIALS

Yardages are based on 42"-wide fabrics.

4⅜ yards of light pink floral for appliqué block backgrounds, pieced blocks, setting blocks, and border

2 yards of green-and-pink floral for pieced blocks and setting blocks

1 yard of green print for stems and leaves, and binding

½ yard of dark pink print for hearts and circles

4⅞ yards of fabric for backing

76" x 88" piece of batting

Mechanical pencil or your favorite wash-out fabric marker

CUTTING

All measurements include ¼"-wide seam allowances.

From the light pink floral, cut:

9 strips, 6" x 42"

7 strips, 6½" x 42"; crosscut into 42 squares, 6½" x 6½"*

6 strips, 7¼" x 42"; crosscut into 30 squares, 7¼" x 7¼". Cut each square twice diagonally to yield 120 triangles.

From the green print, cut:

24 strips, ¾" x 3"

9 yards *total* of 2¼"-wide bias binding strips

From the green-and-pink floral, cut:

3 strips, 6½" x 42"; crosscut into 18 squares, 6½" x 6½"

6 strips, 7¼" x 42"; crosscut into 30 squares, 7¼" x 7¼". Cut each square twice diagonally to yield 120 triangles.

*If you wish, you can cut the 24 squares that will be used for the appliqué blocks 1" larger (7½" x 7½") and trim them to 6½" x 6½" after completing the appliqués.

MAKING THE APPLIQUÉD BLOCKS

1. Fold the light pink 6½" background squares into quarters and gently crease the folds. Match the center folds to the center marks on the full-sized pattern on page 45. Lightly trace the design onto each square.

2. Make appliqué templates for the blocks using the patterns on page 45. Cut and prepare the appliqué pieces from the appropriate fabrics using your favorite method and referring to the photo on page 40 as necessary.

3. Appliqué the pieces for each block to the background squares in numerical order using your favorite appliqué technique. Refer to "Stem Method One" on page 85 to appliqué the green print ¾" x 3" pieces to the squares for the stems and to "Perfect Circles" on page 86 to appliqué the circles above the hearts.

MAKING THE PIECED BLOCKS

1. Sew each light pink floral triangle to a green-and-pink floral triangle along the short edges as shown. Make 120 pieced triangles.

Make 120.

2. Sew two pieced triangles together to make a pieced block. Repeat to make a total of 60 blocks.

Make 60.

ASSEMBLING THE QUILT TOP

Refer to the quilt assembly diagram on page 44, "Straight Sets" on page 89, and "Overlapped Corners" on page 89 to assemble your quilt top.

1. If you cut the background squares oversized, trim them to 6½" square, being careful to center the design in each block.

2. Arrange the appliquéd blocks, pieced blocks, light pink 6½" setting blocks, and green-and-pink 6½" setting blocks into 12 rows of 10 blocks each as shown. Sew the blocks together in rows. Press the seam allowances toward the setting blocks. Sew the rows together. Press the seam allowances in one direction.

3. Sew two light pink 6" x 42" border strips together end to end to make one long strip. Repeat to make a total of two pieced strips. From each pieced strip, cut one strip, 6" x 60½". Sew these strips to the top and bottom of the quilt top.

4. Cut one of the remaining light pink 6" x 42" border strips in half crosswise. Sew one half strip and two full-length border strips together end to end. Repeat to make a total of two pieced strips. From each pieced strip, cut one strip, 6" x 83½". Sew these strips to the sides of the quilt top.

FINISHING THE QUILT

Refer to "Finishing Techniques" on page 91 as needed to complete the following steps.

1. Layer the quilt top with the batting and backing. Baste the layers together.

2. Hand or machine quilt as desired.

3. Square up the quilt sandwich.

4. To round the quilt corners, place a small plate in each corner and draw around the edges. Cut on the marked lines. Prepare and sew the green bias binding strips to the quilt, easing the binding along the outer edge of each corner curve.

5. Add a hanging sleeve, if desired, and a label.

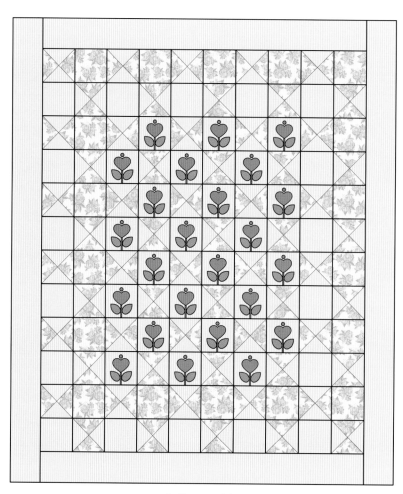

Quilt assembly

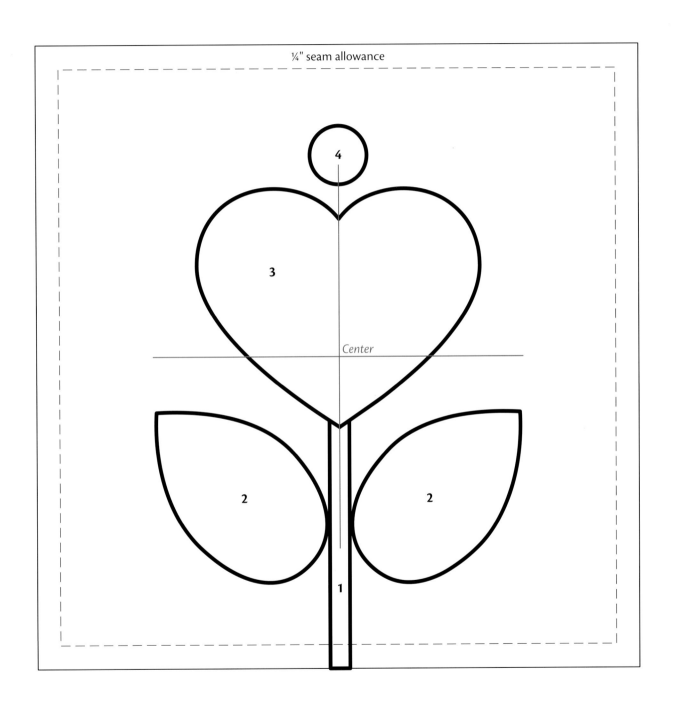

¼" seam allowance

4

3

Center

2

2

1

Hope Blossoms

by Mimi Dietrich

FINISHED QUILT: 34" x 34"

FINISHED BLOCK: 9" x 9"

*Q*uilters make a difference in this world! I am always amazed at the response of quilters when a tragedy occurs. They make quilts for soldiers, quilts for hospitals, quilts for sick children. They make raffle quilts or opportunity quilts to raise money for organizations that support education and research. In all these ways and more, quilters make quilts for other people.

This quilt uses a brighter color palette than "Blossoms of Hope," the original quilt, which was featured in a book called Pink Ribbon Quilts: A Book Because of Breast Cancer. *I wrote the book to celebrate a 5-year anniversary, and now I've celebrated a 10-year one! I received so many wonderful notes and letters about the little quilts in that book; they touched people and helped them stitch through some challenging situations. The quilts brought people together and showed how much they care about each another. The blossoms of hope refer to a hope that we can someday find a cure for breast cancer, but my hope is also that our quilts will always have that special quality that brings people together.*

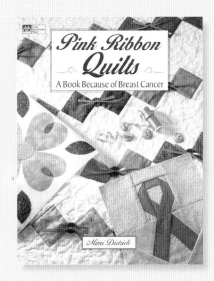

Blossoms of Hope *from* Pink Ribbon Quilts

MATERIALS

Yardages are based on 42"-wide fabrics.

1 yard of blue floral for setting pieces and outer border

⅜ yard of white-on-white print for block backgrounds

⅜ yard of bright pink print for appliqué pieces and inner border

⅜ yard of green print for appliqué pieces and binding

⅛ yard of light pink print for appliqué pieces

⅛ yard of bright yellow print for appliqué pieces

1⅛ yards of fabric for backing

38" x 38" piece of batting

Mechanical pencil or your favorite wash-out fabric marker

CUTTING

All measurements include ¼"-wide seam allowances.

From the white-on-white print, cut:

4 squares, 9½" x 9½"*

From the blue floral, cut:

1 square, 9½" x 9½"

1 square, 14" x 14"; cut twice diagonally to yield 4 triangles

2 squares, 7¼" x 7¼"; cut once diagonally to yield 4 triangles

2 strips, 3½" x 28"

2 strips, 3½" x 34"

From the bright pink print, cut:

2 strips, 1½" x 26"

2 strips, 1½" x 28"

From the green print, cut:

4 binding strips, 2" x 42"

If you wish, you can cut the squares 1" larger (10½" x 10½") and trim them to 9½" x 9½" after completing the appliqués.

APPLIQUÉING THE BLOCKS

1. Fold the white-on-white 9½" background squares *diagonally* into quarters and lightly crease the folds. Match the center folds to the center marks on the full-sized pattern on page 49. Lightly trace the appliqué design onto each square.

2. Make appliqué templates for the blocks using the patterns on page 49. Cut and prepare the appliqué pieces from the appropriate fabrics using your favorite method and referring to the photo on page 46 as necessary.

3. Appliqué the pieces for each block to the background squares in numerical order using your favorite appliqué technique. Do not turn under the center edges of the piece 1 appliqués. They will be covered by the center circle. Refer to "Perfect Circles" on page 86 to appliqué the center circles.

ASSEMBLING THE QUILT TOP

Refer to the photo on page 46, "Diagonal Sets" on page 89, and "Overlapped Corners" on page 89 to assemble your quilt top.

1. If you cut the background squares oversized, trim them to 9½" square, being careful to center the design in each block.

2. Arrange the appliquéd blocks, the blue 9½" setting square, and the blue setting triangles as shown. Sew the blocks and triangles together to form diagonal rows. Press the seam allowances toward the blue pieces. Join the rows, adding the corner setting triangles last. Press the seam allowances in one direction.

3. Sew the bright pink 1½" x 26" inner-border strips to the sides of the quilt top. Sew the bright pink 1½" x 28" inner-border strips to the top and bottom of the quilt top.

4. Sew the blue 3½" x 28" outer-border strips to the sides of the quilt top. Sew the blue 3½" x 34" outer-border strips to the top and bottom of the quilt top.

FINISHING THE QUILT

Refer to "Finishing Techniques" on page 91 as needed to complete the following steps.

1. Layer the quilt top with the batting and backing. Baste the layers together.

2. Hand or machine quilt as desired.

3. Square up the quilt sandwich.

4. Prepare and sew the green binding strips to the quilt. Add a hanging sleeve, if desired, and a label.

Yo-Yo Berries

by Eleanor Eckman

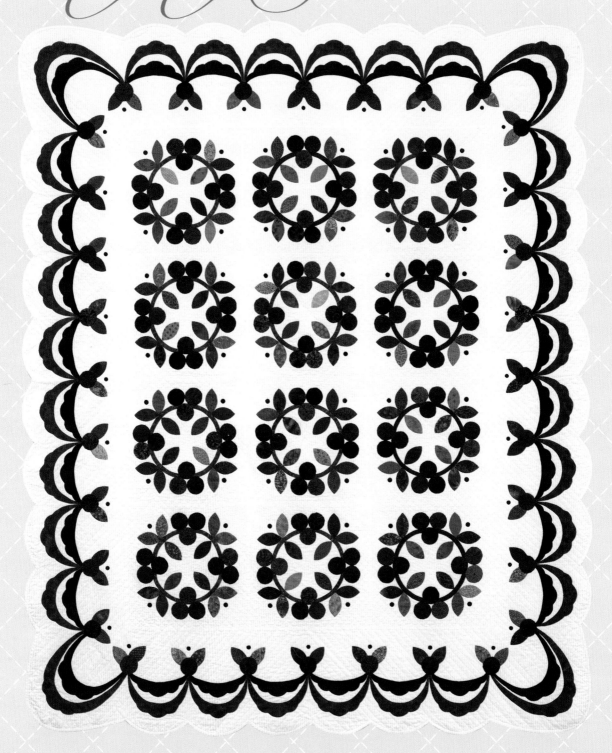

FINISHED QUILT: 75½" x 91½"

FINISHED BLOCK: 16" x 16"

*W*hat inspires you to quilt? I'm inspired by traditional quilts. My great grandmother made quilts in Mississippi in the 1930s. I slept under one of these quilts when I was growing up, so there is a special place in my heart for 1930s quilts. When I made "Garden Comfort" for my book Bed and Breakfast Quilts, I chose 1930s reproduction fabrics for the color palette. Something about the round flowers made me think of the dimensional yo-yos on many of the old quilts, so yo-yos became the appliquéd flowers. When Eleanor Eckman made "Yo-Yo Berries," she used a variety of red and green fabrics from a fabric swap in my "Graduate Class" and added a traditional appliqué swag border. It completely changes the look of the quilt and gives it a Baltimore touch. It's fun to see two quilts inspired by the same design—they show how we look at things in different ways. I am always thrilled when my students use my designs and make them their own!

Garden Comfort *from* Bed and Breakfast Quilts

Yo-Yo Berries

MATERIALS

Yardages are based on 42"-wide fabrics.

9¼ yards of white-on-white print for blocks, border, and binding

3¼ yards *total* of assorted red prints for yo-yo circles and small circles

2 yards *total* of assorted green prints for leaves

2 yards of dark green print for border swags

¾ yard of medium green print for wreath stems

1¼ yards of red print for border swags

5⅝ yards of white fabric for backing

80" x 96" piece of batting

Mechanical pencil or your favorite wash-out fabric marker

Water-soluble marker

Template plastic or compact disc

CUTTING

All measurements include ¼"-wide seam allowances.

From the white-on-white print, cut:

12 squares, 16½" x 16½"*

2 strips, 14" x 77½", along the *lengthwise* grain

2 strips, 14" x 93½", along the *lengthwise* grain

9½ yards *total* of 2¼"-wide bias binding strips

From medium green print, cut:

12 bias strips, 1" x 33"

*If you wish, you can cut the squares 1" larger (17½" x 17½") and trim them to 16½" x 16½" after completing the appliqués.

APPLIQUÉING THE BLOCKS

1. Make four photocopies of the quarter-block wreath pattern on page 55. Tape the copies together as shown to make a full-sized wreath pattern.

2. Fold the white-on-white background squares into quarters and gently crease the folds. Lightly trace the full-sized pattern onto each square, matching the center folds to the center mark on the pattern.

3. Make appliqué templates for the blocks using the full-sized patterns on page 55. Cut and prepare the leaf and small circle pieces from the appropriate appliqué fabrics using your favorite method and referring to the photo on page 50 as necessary.

4. Fold the long edges of the medium green bias stems into the center of the strip, wrong sides together, so that the raw edges meet. Baste along both edges of each strip with small stitches. Gently pull on one of the basting threads to ease each bias strip into a curve.

Pull thread to create curve.

5. Appliqué the pieces for each block to the background squares in numerical order using your favorite appliqué technique. For the wreath stems, position the ends where they will be covered by a yo-yo flower, folding each end under ¼" to finish the edges. Refer to "Perfect Circles" on page 86 for the berries.

Fold ends of stem
under ¼".

MAKING THE YO-YO FLOWERS

1. Make a 4¾"-diameter template from template plastic or use a compact disc (for music or computer) as your template. Use the template to mark 176 circles onto the wrong side of the assorted red prints. Cut out the circles exactly on the marked lines.

2. For each yo-yo, turn under ¼" around the outside edge of the circle, folding the wrong sides together.

3. Using a doubled length of thread about 20" long, sew a running stitch around the outside of the circle. Start stitching on the right side of the circle and leave a tail so you can tie a knot later.

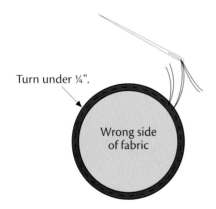

Turn under ¼".

Wrong side
of fabric

4. When you have stitched all the way around the circle, take your last stitch next to the first one on the right side. Pull the threads to gather the edges into the center of the circle.

5. Tie the tails into a knot. Pinch the gathers together and tie a few more knots to hold them tight. Thread the tails into the needle and stitch into the gathers of the yo-yo to hide the ends.

6. Appliqué the edges of the yo-yo circles to the wreaths. Reserve the remaining yo-yos for the border.

APPLIQUÉING THE BORDER

1. Fold each border strip in half crosswise and mark the center with the water-soluble marker. On the white-on-white 77½"-long borders, measure and mark three 8" spaces on both sides of the center mark. On the white-on-white 93½"-long borders, measure and mark four 8" spaces on both sides of the center mark. Mark an X on each line, 6" from the inner-border edge.

Center

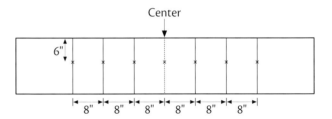

6"

8" 8" 8" 8" 8" 8"

2. Make appliqué templates for the swags using the full-sized patterns on pages 56 and 57. Cut and prepare the swag pieces from the appropriate appliqué fabrics using your favorite method and referring to the photo on page 50 as necessary.

3. Appliqué the red inner swags and then the green outer swags to each border strip, matching the points to the Xs marked on the strips. Appliqué six swag sets to the shorter strips and eight sets to the longer strips.

4. Appliqué two leaves and a yo-yo over the points of all of the swags, except those at the end of each strip. These will be applied after the borders are attached to the quilt top.

5. Appliqué a small circle above each yo-yo, 2¾" from the inner-border edge.

ASSEMBLING THE QUILT TOP

Refer to the quilt assembly diagram below, "Straight Sets" on page 89, and "Mitered Corners" on page 90 to assemble your quilt top.

1. If you cut the background squares oversized, trim them to 16½" square, being careful to center the design in each block.

2. Arrange the wreath blocks into four rows of three blocks each. Sew the blocks together in each row. Press the seam allowances in opposite directions from row to row. Sew the rows together. Press the seam allowances in one direction.

3. Sew the white-on-white 14" x 93½"-long border strips to the sides of the quilt top and the white-on-white 14" x 77½" border strips to the top and bottom of the quilt top, mitering the corners.

Quilt assembly

4. Appliqué the corner border swags to the corners of the quilt.

5. Appliqué the remaining yo-yos, leaves, and small circles to each swag point as you did previously.

6. To mark the scalloped edge, use the water-soluble marker to mark a dot 1½" from the raw edges of the quilt, directly across from each yo-yo. Draw a curve from dot to dot that touches the outer edge of the quilt at the curve's outermost point. Round off the corners of the quilt. Do not trim the curves until you have applied the binding.

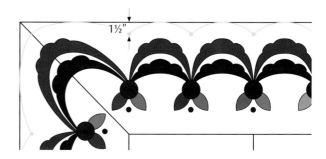

1½"

FINISHING THE QUILT

Refer to "Finishing Techniques" on page 91 as needed to complete the following steps.

1. Layer the quilt top with the batting and backing. Baste the layers together.

2. Hand or machine quilt as desired.

3. Prepare and sew the white-on-white bias binding strips to the quilt. Ease the binding along the outer edge of each curve. At each inner point, leave the needle in the fabric, pivot, turn the binding to match the next curve, and continue sewing the next curve. Trim the edge of the quilt even with the binding when you are finished sewing it in place. Turn the binding to the back of the quilt and stitch it in place, folding a miter in the binding at each inner point.

4. Add a hanging sleeve, if desired, and a label.

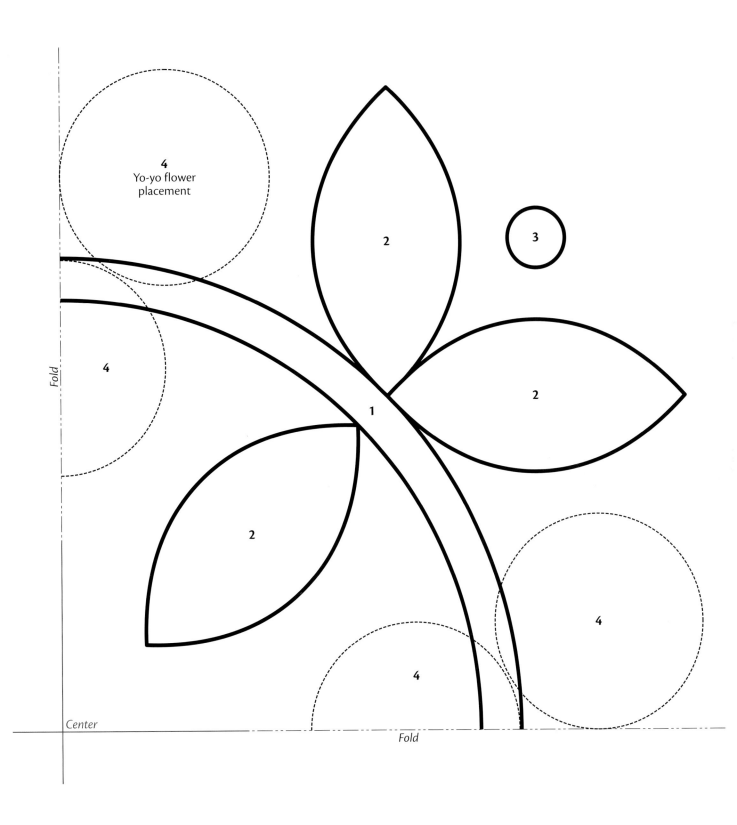

4
Yo-yo flower
placement

3

2

Fold

4

2

1

2

4

2

4

Center

Fold

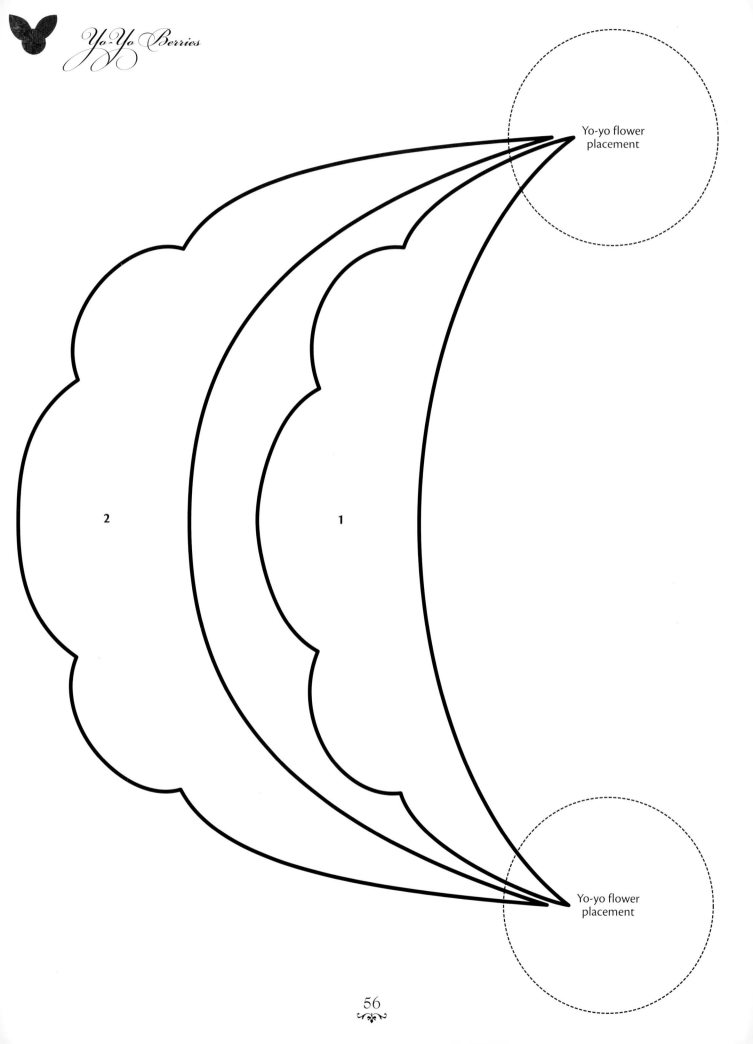

Yo-yo flower
placement

2

1

Yo-yo flower
placement

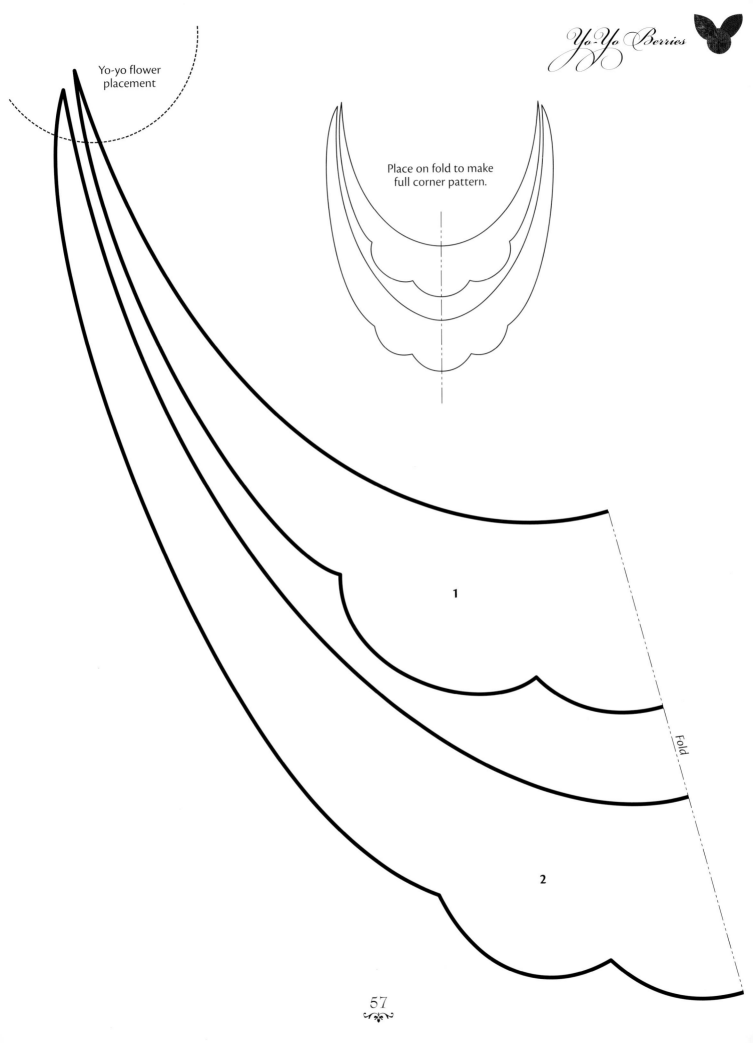

Yo-yo flower
placement

Place on fold to make
full corner pattern.

1

Fold

2

Mini Mimi

by Mimi Dietrich

FINISHED QUILT: 25" x 27⅞"

FINISHED BLOCK: 2" x 2"

I made my first quilts during the bicentennial of the United States when many magazines featured photos of traditional quilts. Twenty years later, I worked with the Smithsonian Institution to publish new quilt patterns inspired by the antique quilts in the museum. I love traditional quilts, I love old fabrics and patterns, and I love the soft colors of reproduction fabrics.

"Vintage Memories," which inspired this mini-quilt, combines traditional four-patch designs and reproduction fabrics. It was made by a group of friends in Iowa who collect vintage and reproduction fabrics. I sent them the background fabric, and they used their collection to bring the quilt to life. Imagine my surprise when the mailman brought me a little box of 1½" square scraps and a pattern for "Mini Mimi." We all have one of these small quilts to remind us of the large one, which was raffled to benefit the textile collection of the Grout Museum in Waterloo, Iowa.

Vintage Memories *from* Bed and Breakfast Quilts

MATERIALS

Yardages are based on 42"-wide fabrics.

1⅛ yards of light tan print for setting squares, setting triangles, and outer border

¼ yard of medium green print for vines and stems

⅛ yard of plum print for inner borders

Scraps of assorted prints for pieced blocks and appliqué pieces

¼ yard of dark green print for binding

1 yard of fabric for backing

29" x 32" piece of batting

Mechanical pencil or your favorite wash-out fabric marker

48 pink buttons, ¼"-diameter

CUTTING

All measurements include ¼"-wide seam allowances.

From the assorted prints, cut a *total* of:

60 pairs of squares, 1½" x 1½"

From the light tan print, cut:

2 strips, 5" x 25"

2 strips, 5" x 18⅞"

2 strips, 2½" x 42"; crosscut into 20 squares, 2½" x 2½"

1 strip, 4⅞" x 42"; crosscut into 5 squares, 4⅞" x 4⅞". Cut each square twice diagonally to yield 18 side setting triangles (there will be 2 extra triangles).

2 squares, 2¾" x 2¾"; cut once diagonally to yield 4 corner setting triangles

From the plum print, cut:

2 strips, 1" x 17⅞"

2 strips, 1" x 16"

From the medium green print, cut:

3½ yards *total* of ½"-wide bias strips

From the dark green print, cut:

3 binding strips, 2" x 42"

MAKING THE BLOCKS

1. Select two pairs of 1½" squares that make a pleasing combination. Sew the squares together. Press the seam allowances toward the darker fabric. Repeat to make 30 sets of pairs.

2. Sew each set of squares together as shown to make a pieced block.

Make 30.

ASSEMBLING THE QUILT TOP

Refer to the quilt assembly diagram below, "Diagonal Sets" on page 89, and "Overlapped Corners" on page 89 to assemble your quilt top.

1. Arrange the pieced blocks, light tan 2½" setting squares, and setting triangles as shown. Sew the blocks and triangles together to form diagonal rows. (The setting triangles are oversized and will be trimmed later.) Press the seam allowances toward the setting squares and triangles. Join the rows, adding the corner setting triangles last. Press the seam allowances in one direction.

2. Trim the quilt edges ½" from the block points.

3. Sew the plum 1" x 17⅞" inner-border strips to the sides of the quilt top. Sew the plum 1" x 16" inner-border strips to the top and bottom of the quilt top.

4. Sew the light tan 5" x 18⅞" outer-border strips to the sides of the quilt top. Sew the light tan 5" x 25" outer-border strips to the top and bottom of the quilt top.

Quilt assembly

APPLIQUÉING THE BORDER

1. Enlarge the border pattern on page 63 to 200%. The pattern will require more than one piece of paper; tape the papers together to make a complete pattern.

2. Fold the quilt into quarters. Match the center folds on the quilt edges to the center marks on the border patterns. Trace the border appliqué design onto one quarter of the border. Flip the pattern over and use a light box (or tape the pattern and quilt to a sunny window), and trace the other half of the pattern.

3. Make appliqué templates for the border using the enlarged patterns. Cut and prepare the appliqué pieces from the appropriate appliqué fabrics using your favorite method and referring to the photo on page 58 as necessary. If you use the freezer-paper appliqué method on page 83, trace the bird bodies in reverse.

4. Appliqué the pieces to the border in numerical order using your favorite appliqué technique. Refer to "Stem Method One" on page 85 to appliqué the short stems; then appliqué the long stems, starting and stopping under the flowers and pineapple leaves.

5. Refer to the photo to sew the buttons next to the short stems.

FINISHING THE QUILT

Refer to "Finishing Techniques" on page 91 as needed to complete the following steps.

1. Layer the quilt top with the batting and backing. Baste the layers together.

2. Hand or machine quilt as desired.

3. Square up the quilt sandwich.

4. Prepare and sew the green binding strips to the quilt. Add a hanging sleeve, if desired, and a label.

Center

Enlarge patterns 200%.

Button placement

Center

¼" seam allowance

Angels of Comfort

by Mimi Dietrich, machine quilted by Linda Newsom

FINISHED QUILT: 35⁷/₈" x 35⁷/₈"

FINISHED BLOCK: 8" x 8"

*Q*uilts provide comfort in many ways. When we dream of quilt ideas, we feel inspired. When we create and sew quilts, we often feel soothed. When we give quilts to others, the comfort they feel from our gift is often matched by the warm glow it gives us to know we have done something nice for someone else.

Sometimes we find comfort in expressing our creativity. When I was a young mother with two boys, I enjoyed spending a few moments sewing each day. I loved the solitude, I loved to create, and I loved doing something that would remain "done," unlike the clean clothes or swept floors. I could curl up with a quilt around me at the end of a long day and enjoy the feeling of accomplishment in the stitches. Many women experience hand appliqué or quilting as a form of meditation. There's a calming effect in the repetition of the stitches.

May these angels bring you faith, hope, love, and the comfort you need as you stitch them.

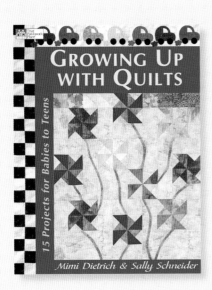

May Angels Watch Over You *from* Growing Up with Quilts

MATERIALS

Yardages are based on 42"-wide fabrics.

1⅝ yards of aqua batik print for setting square, setting triangles, and outer border

1 yard of dark aqua print for appliqué block backgrounds, inner border, letters, and binding

⅛ yard of tan checked fabric (or desired color) for face and feet

⅛ yard of light brown print (or desired color) for hair

Scraps of assorted pink, green, purple and yellow fabrics for hearts, dresses, and pocket hankies

1¼ yards of fabric for backing

40" x 40" piece of batting

Mechanical pencil or your favorite wash-out fabric marker

4 scalloped doilies (4" to 6" diameter) for angel wings

Embroidery floss: dark brown, dark aqua, and white

Hand-sewing needles: size 8 embroidery; size 10 Sharp

8 small black beads for angel eyes; approximately 100 white seed beads for halos

Assorted small buttons for embellishment

CUTTING

All measurements include ¼"-wide seam allowances.

From the dark aqua print, cut:

4 squares, 8½" x 8½"*

2 strips, 1¾" x 23⅜"

2 strips, 1¾" x 25⅞"

4 binding strips, 2" x 42"

From the assorted fabric scraps, cut:

4 squares, 1½" x 1½"

From the light brown print, cut:

4 strips, 1⅛" x 14"

From the aqua batik print, cut:

2 strips, 5½" x 25⅞"

2 strips, 5½" x 35⅞"

1 square, 8½" x 8½"

1 square, 12⅝" x 12⅝"; cut twice diagonally to yield 4 side setting triangles

2 squares, 6⅝" x 6⅝"; cut once diagonally to yield 4 corner setting triangles

If you wish, you can cut the squares 1" larger (9½" x 9½") and trim them to 8½" x 8½" after completing the appliqués.

APPLIQUÉING THE BLOCKS

1. Fold the dark aqua 8½" background squares *diagonally* into quarters and gently crease the folds. Match the center folds to the center marks on the full-sized pattern on page 70. Lightly trace the appliqué design onto each square, reversing two.

2. Make appliqué templates for the blocks using the patterns on page 70. Cut and prepare the appliqué pieces from the appropriate appliqué fabrics using your favorite method and referring to the photo on page 64 as necessary. Cut pieces 3 and 5 in reverse for the two angels on the right-hand side of the quilt. If you use the freezer-paper appliqué method described on page 83, trace two angels in reverse.

3. Place a doily in the wing area of each marked block as shown. Appliqué the two top scallops. Trim the excess doily so that it extends into the dress area ¼".

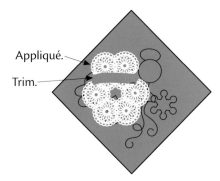

Appliqué.

Trim.

4. Appliqué pieces 1–6 to the background squares in numerical order using your favorite appliqué technique.

5. Appliqué the curved edge of piece 7 to each square. Fold the pocket hanky squares as shown. Tuck the raw edges of each hanky into a pocket, and then appliqué across the top of the pocket to secure it.

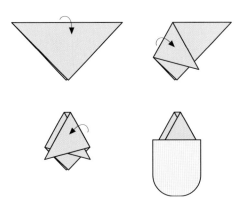

6. Fold the long edges of each light brown strip into the center of the strip, wrong sides together, so that the raw edges meet; press.

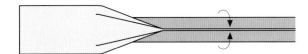

7. Lay each strip right side up along the ruching guide below. Transfer the marks on the guide to each strip. Hand sew a running stitch from mark to mark as shown.

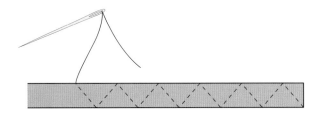

Ruching guide for angel hair

8. Pull the thread to gather the fabric into a 4"-long strip, leaving ¼" not gathered at each end. Fold the tails under, and then appliqué the edges around each angel's head as shown.

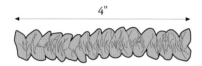

9. Referring to "Embroidery Stitches" on page 88, use two strands of dark brown embroidery floss to blanket stitch around the outside of each appliqué (except for the hair and wings). Using two strands of white embroidery floss and a chain stitch, embroider the swirls.

10. Thread the Sharp needle with sewing thread to match the beads. Stitch the seed beads to the halo lines, bringing the needle up at the bead location, and then through the bead, and back down through the fabric close to where the needle came out.

11. Sew two black beads to each angel's face where indicated for the eyes. Refer to the photo on page 64 to add small button embellishments to the arms and swirls.

APPLIQUÉING THE BORDER

1. Enlarge the patterns on page 71 to 200%. Using the enlarged patterns, make appliqué templates for the outer border. Cut and prepare each letter from the remaining dark aqua print using your favorite method.

2. Center the letters for each word on the aqua batik outer-border strips, positioning the letters 1¼" from the raw edges. "Faith" and "Comfort" should be on the longer strips, "Hope" and "Love" on the shorter strips. Appliqué the letters in place using your favorite appliqué technique. Using two strands of dark aqua embroidery floss, blanket stitch around the outside of each letter.

Mix It Up!

Even if you have hand-appliquéd the angels on your quilt, it's OK to use a different technique for the letters on the border. Follow the instructions on your favorite fusible web, and iron the letters and hearts to the borders, making sure you reverse the letters when you trace the shapes onto the fusible web. You can even machine buttonhole stitch around the edges!

3. Using the heart template you made in step 1 of "Appliquéing the Blocks," cut and prepare eight hearts from pink scraps and appliqué one on each side of the border words. Position the hearts 1" from the letters and 1¾" from the border outer edge. Outline each heart with dark aqua embroidery floss and a blanket stitch.

ASSEMBLING THE QUILT TOP

Refer to the quilt assembly diagram below, "Diagonal Sets" on page 89, and "Overlapped Corners" on page 89 to assemble your quilt top.

1. If you cut the background squares oversized, trim them to 8½" square, being careful to center the design in each block.

2. Arrange the Angel blocks and the aqua batik setting square and setting triangles as shown. Sew the blocks and triangles together to form diagonal rows. Join the rows, adding the corner setting triangles last.

3. Sew the dark aqua 1¾" x 23⅜" inner-border strips to the sides of the quilt top. Sew the dark aqua 1¾" x 25⅞" inner-border strips to the top and bottom of the quilt top.

4. Sew the aqua batik 5½" x 25⅞" outer-border strips to the sides of the quilt top. Sew the aqua batik 5½" x 35⅞" outer-border strips to the top and bottom of the quilt top.

FINISHING THE QUILT

Refer to "Finishing Techniques" on page 91 as needed to complete the following steps.

1. Layer the quilt top with the batting and backing. Baste the layers together.

2. Hand or machine quilt as desired.

3. Square up the quilt sandwich.

4. Prepare and sew the dark aqua binding strips to the quilt. Add a hanging sleeve, if desired, and a label.

Quilt assembly

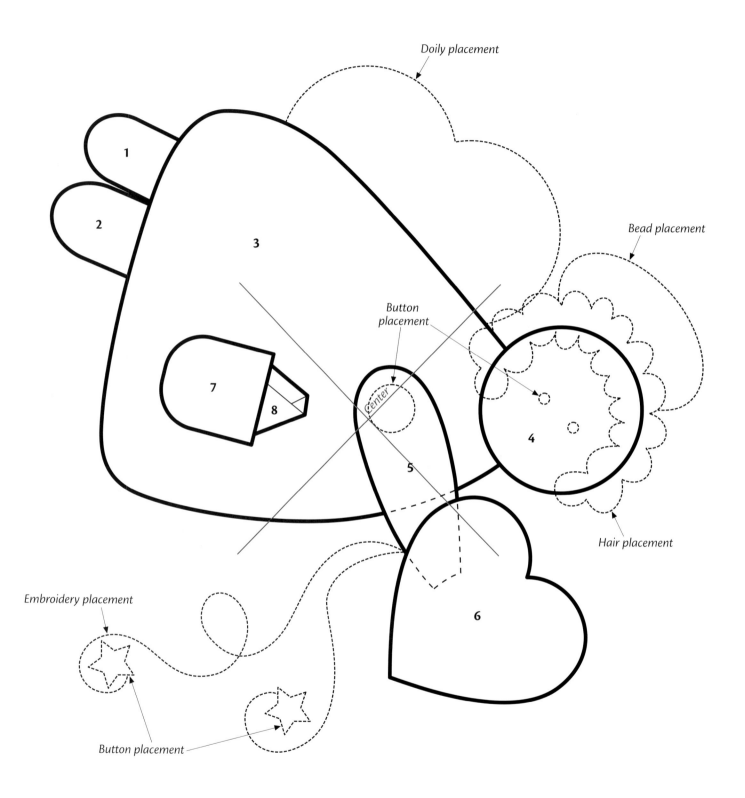

Doily placement

Bead placement

Button
placement

Hair placement

Embroidery placement

Button placement

Center

1

2

3

4

5

6

7

8

FAITH

LOVE

HOPE

COMFORT

Enlarge patterns 200%.

Appliqué Sampler

by Mimi Dietrich

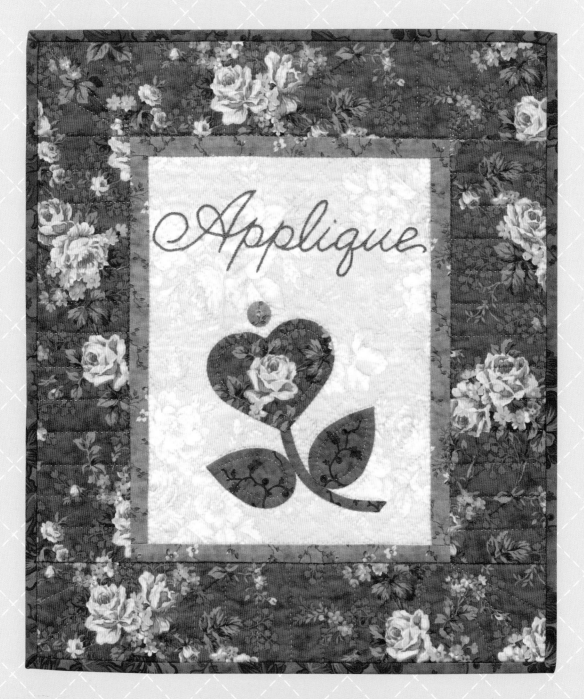

FINISHED QUILT: 16½" x 19½"
FINISHED BLOCK: 9" x 12"

I look forward to trying new things: new colors, new techniques, and new designs! But I like to try them on small projects. Of all the books I have authored, one of my favorites is Easy Appliqué Samplers, *a collection of small projects inspired by antique needlework samplers. The projects were designed so that students could sample different appliqué techniques—hand appliqué, machine appliqué, freezer-paper templates, and needle-turn stitching. It's fun to try a new idea for a project or to try different techniques within one project—you never know when you'll find a technique that is just right for a new project. Trying new techniques also helps you decide which ones you really like. So try something new when you stitch the flower on this "sampler," and finish it off with one of my favorite things—appliqué—embroidered with a chain stitch.*

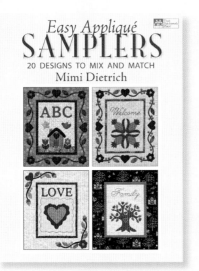

ABC Sampler *from* Easy Appliqué Samplers

MATERIALS

Yardages are based on 42"-wide fabrics.

⅜ yard of large-scale pink floral for appliqué pieces and outer border

⅓ yard of tan-on-tan print for appliqué block background

¼ yard of small-scale blue floral for appliqué pieces and inner border

¼ yard of green print for appliqué pieces and binding

⅝ yard of fabric for backing

21" x 24" piece of batting

Mechanical pencil or your favorite wash-out fabric marker

Blue embroidery floss

Size 8 embroidery needle

CUTTING

All measurements include ¼"-wide seam allowances.

From the tan-on-tan print, cut:

1 rectangle, 9½" x 12½"*

From the small-scale blue floral, cut:

2 strips, 1" x 10½"

2 strips, 1" x 12½"

From the large-scale pink floral, cut:

2 strips, 3½" x 13½"

2 strips, 3½" x 16½"

From the green print, cut:

1 bias strip, ⅝" x 4½"

2 binding strips, 2" x 42"

*If you wish, you can cut the rectangle 1" larger (10½" x 13½") and trim it to 9½" x 12½" after completing the appliqués.

APPLIQUÉING THE BLOCK

1. Fold the background rectangle into quarters and gently crease the folds. Match the center folds to the center marks on the full-sized pattern on page 76. Lightly trace the design onto the rectangle.

2. Match the top raw edge of the background rectangle to the top of the pattern and trace the lettering.

3. Make appliqué templates for the block using the patterns on page 76. Cut and prepare the appliqué pieces from the appropriate appliqué fabrics using your favorite method and referring to the photo on page 72 as necessary.

4. Appliqué the pieces to the background rectangle in numerical order using your favorite appliqué technique and referring to "Stem Method One" on page 85 to appliqué the stem. Let the stem's top edge lie flat over the placement lines for the heart, but turn under the bottom edge.

5. Refer to "Embroidery Stitches" on page 88 to chain stitch the lettering with two strands of blue embroidery floss and the embroidery needle.

ASSEMBLING THE QUILT TOP

Refer to the quilt assembly diagram below and "Overlapped Corners" on page 89 to assemble your quilt top.

1. If you cut the background rectangle oversized, trim it to 9½" x 12½", being careful to center the design in the block.

2. Sew the blue 1" x 12½" inner-border strips to the sides of the quilt top. Sew the blue 1" x 10½" inner-border strips to the top and bottom of the quilt top.

3. Sew the pink 3½" x 13½" outer-border strips to the sides of the quilt top. Sew the pink 3½" x 16½" outer-border strips to the top and bottom of the quilt top.

FINISHING THE QUILT

Refer to "Finishing Techniques" on page 91 as needed to complete the following steps.

1. Layer the quilt top with the batting and backing. Baste the layers together.

2. Hand or machine quilt as desired.

3. Square up the quilt sandwich.

4. Prepare and sew the green binding strips to the quilt. Add a hanging sleeve, if desired, and a label.

Quilt assembly

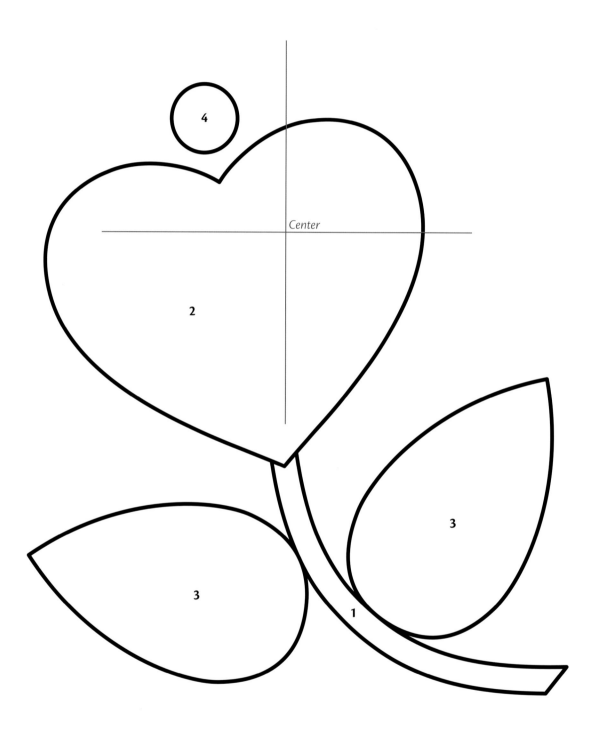

Align dashed line with raw edge of top of 9½" x 12½" rectangle.

Applique

Monogram Wreath

by Mimi Dietrich

FINISHED QUILT: 26½" x 26½"

FINISHED BLOCK: 12" x 12"

I love to appliqué! I also love to sew by machine, but I really *love* to hand appliqué. Even though the current trend in quilting leans toward machine work and getting projects finished quickly, I prefer to sit in my favorite chair and appliqué by hand. I enjoy touching the fabrics and seeing the progress with each stitch. It's important to be true to your feelings and ideals and to find a little time each day to feed your soul.

When you make a quilt, add something special to make it your own! We all use patterns or traditional designs, but it's fun to include a personal touch. I've always liked monograms, and I found this traditional Baltimore-style wreath to be the perfect place to appliqué the letters. I originally made this block for the center of a full-size Baltimore Album quilt, but it also looks great as a one-block wall hanging.

MATERIALS

Yardages are based on 42"-wide fabrics.

1 yard of red floral for setting triangles, outer border, and binding

½ yard of light tan print for appliqué block background

¼ yard of blue print for appliqué pieces and inner border

¼ yard of dark tan print for vines

⅛ yard of white solid for dimensional flowers

5" x 10" rectangle of medium green Ultrasuede for first and middle initial monograms

5" square of dark green Ultrasuede for last initial monogram

Scraps of assorted red and green prints for berries and leaves

⅞ yard of fabric for backing

31" x 31" piece of batting

Mechanical pencil or your favorite wash-out fabric marker

Fabric glue stick

Size 11 Sharp or milliner's needle

60-weight cotton or silk thread to match monogram fabrics

24 brown seed beads for flower centers

CUTTING

All measurements include ¼"-wide seam allowances.

From the light tan print, cut:

1 square, 12½" x 12½"*

From the dark tan print, cut:

2 bias strips, ½" x 10"

From the white solid, cut:

8 circles, 2½"-diameter (template on page 87)

From the red floral, cut:

2 squares, 9⅜" x 9⅜"; cut once diagonally to yield 4 triangles

2 strips, 4" x 19½"

2 strips, 4" x 26½"

3 binding strips, 2" x 42"

From the blue print, cut:

2 strips, 1½" x 17½"

2 strips, 1½" x 19½"

If you wish, you can cut the square 1" larger (13½" x 13½") and trim it to 12½" x 12½" after completing the appliqués.

Glorious Girl

by Mimi Dietrich, machine quilted by Linda Newsom

This quilt was inspired by a novel called The Secret Life of Bees. *I just loved the characters, wonderful women who supported each other through life. The sentence "Get up from there and live like the glorious girl you are" just spoke to me! I think of myself and my friends as "glorious girls," even though some younger people might consider us a little more mature. I wanted to make a quilt with this sentence in the border—that's how the quilt got started. Then I collected some favorite fabrics, especially the honey yellow colors, and just let them sit in my studio and inspire me.*

FINISHED QUILT: 35⅞" x 35⅞"
FINISHED BLOCK: 12" x 12"

The big moment came, however, when I was in a quilt shop and saw the Honeybee block pinned to a wall. Ta-da! That's when I started cutting the fabric! When I was finished, I realized I needed a free-form vine with some leaves and hearts, just because I enjoy appliqué. I started to hand quilt and then decided that my friend Linda Newsom could machine quilt the center better than I could. I like to look at this quilt when I get up in the morning. Its sunny colors and encouraging words help me to "Get up!" start my day, and try to be glorious.

There is no pattern or instruction for this quilt. I will only tell you that the Honeybee blocks are 12" square and the appliquéd hearts, leaves, and honeybee wings are shapes from "Appliqué Sampler" on page 72. I encourage you to find your inspiration—in nature, in literature, in your life. Use your favorite techniques and skills. If you can't do part of it, ask for help from a friend. Make a quilt just because you have to, because your soul is speaking to you, because you are inspired!

Quiltmaking Techniques

There are many ways to make a quilt! Refer to this section of the book for some of my favorite basic quiltmaking techniques. If you would like more details about appliqué techniques, please refer to any of my previous books (see the bibliography on page 95).

APPLIQUÉ QUILTS

In an appliquéd quilt, appliqué fabrics are applied on top of background fabric instead of pieced together to make patchwork patterns.

Background Fabric

The background fabric for appliqué is usually cut in a square. If the finished size of an appliqué block is 9" square, the block needs to be cut 9½" square to allow for seam allowances. Sometimes it is better to cut the square 1" larger to start, and then trim it to the correct size after the appliqué has been completed. Appliqué squares may be cut easily with a large square acrylic ruler and a rotary cutter.

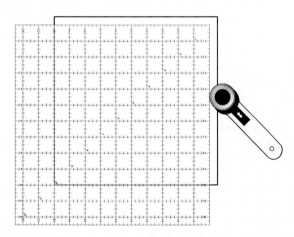

To place the appliqué pieces on the background fabric accurately, I mark the design on the fabric using a silver marking pencil. Place the fabric right

side up over the pattern so that the design is centered. Trace the design carefully. The marks will be dark enough to see and will wash out after the quilt is completed. If your background fabric is too dark and you can't see the pattern clearly, you may need to trace it over a light box or against a sunny window.

Preparing Appliqués with Freezer Paper

Before sewing the appliqué fabrics to the background fabric, you should prepare the appliqués so that the seam allowances are turned under smoothly. This will help you place the appliqués accurately on the marked background fabric. I like to use freezer-paper templates to help make perfectly shaped appliqués.

1. Place the freezer paper, plastic-coated side down, on your pattern, and then trace the design with a sharp pencil. For repeated designs, such as flowers and leaves, make a plastic template and trace around it onto the freezer paper. If the design is asymmetrical (such as the birds in "Bright Songs" on page 32), trace the pattern onto the freezer paper in reverse.

2. Cut out the freezer-paper shape on the pencil line. Do not add seam allowances.

3. Place the plastic-coated side of the freezer paper against the wrong side of the appliqué fabric. Iron the freezer paper to the wrong side of the fabric using a dry, hot iron.

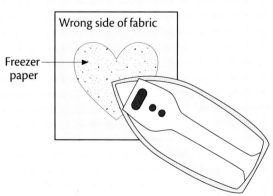

Wrong side of fabric

Freezer paper

4. Cut out the appliqué shape, adding a ¼"-wide seam allowance around the outside of the freezer paper.

5. Baste the seam allowance over the freezer-paper edges, sewing through the paper and two layers of fabric. Clip any inside points and fold outside points.

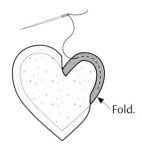

Fold.

6. Pin or baste the appliqué to the background fabric.

7. Stitch the appliqué to the background fabric using the traditional appliqué stitch, described at right.

8. After the shape has been appliquéd, remove any basting stitches. Then cut a small slit in the background fabric behind the appliqué and remove the freezer paper with tweezers.

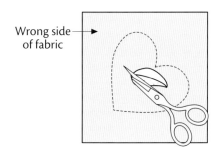

Wrong side of fabric

9. Press the appliqué from the wrong side to avoid flattening it too much.

Traditional Appliqué Stitch

The traditional appliqué stitch is appropriate for sewing all areas of appliqué designs, including sharp points and curves.

1. Thread your needle with a single strand of thread approximately 18" long, and tie a knot in one end. To hide your knot when you start, slip your needle into the seam allowance from the wrong side of the appliqué piece, bringing it out along the fold line. The knot will be hidden inside the seam allowance.

2. Stitch along the top edge of the appliqué. If you are right-handed, stitch from right to left. If you are left-handed, stitch from left to right. Start the first stitch by moving your needle straight off the appliqué, inserting the needle into the background fabric.

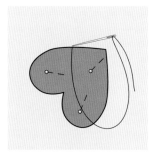

3. Let the needle travel under the background fabric, parallel to the edge of the appliqué, bringing it up about ⅛" away from the last stitch along the pattern line. As you bring the needle back up, pierce the edge of the appliqué piece, catching only one or two threads of the folded edge.

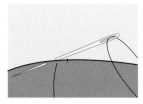

4. Move the needle straight off the appliqué into the background fabric. Let your needle travel under the background, bringing it up about ⅛" away from the last stitch, again catching the edge of the appliqué. Give the thread a slight tug and continue

stitching. The only visible parts of the stitch are very small dots of thread along the appliqué edge.

The part of the stitch that travels forward will be seen as ⅛" stitches on the wrong side of the background fabric. Try to keep the length of your stitches consistent as you stitch along the straight edges. Smaller stitches are sometimes necessary for curves and points.

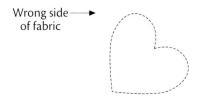

Wrong side of fabric →

Appliqué Stems

I use two different methods for creating appliqué stems. If the stems are straight, you can cut them on the straight grain of the fabric. If the stems curve, you'll need to cut them on the bias. Cut bias strips by measuring an equal distance from a corner along adjacent sides of your fabric. Place your ruler on these measurements and make a diagonal cut. Then align your ruler with the desired strip width and cut strips.

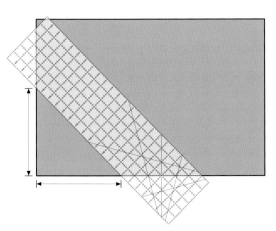

Stem Method One

I love to use this method for stems, especially if they are curved.

1. Cut fabric strips that measure twice the finished stem width. For example, for a ¼" stem, cut the strips ½" wide.

2. Cut these strips into pieces ½" longer than the stem design on the pattern. This allows a ¼"-wide seam allowance at each end, to be covered by leaves or flowers.

3. Fold both raw edges in to meet at the center, wrong sides together. Baste along the folded edges using small running stitches.

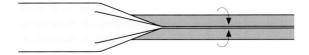

4. Position the strip on the marked stem line of your design, wrong side against the background fabric, and pin or baste the stems to the background fabric. Appliqué along both folded edges. When a stem is long, I use a fabric glue stick to temporarily adhere it to the background fabric to keep it in place while I'm stitching.

5. Remove the basting threads after the stitching is complete.

Stem Method Two

I like to use this method for very thin stems.

1. Cut fabric strips that measure four times the finished stem width. For example, for a ⅛" stem, cut the strips ½" wide.

2. Cut these strips into pieces ½" longer than the stem design on the pattern. This allows a ¼"-wide seam allowance at each end, to be covered by leaves or flowers.

3. Fold the strip in half lengthwise, wrong sides together. Press with a steam iron or baste close to the raw edges.

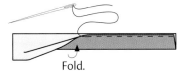

Fold.

4. Position the strip with the raw edges touching one of the marked stem lines. The folded edge of the stem should cover the other line. If the stems curve, as in a wreath shape, position the raw edges of the strip touching the outer curved line.

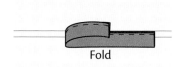

Fold

5. Using small running stitches, sew the strip to the background almost through the center of the strip, slightly closer to the raw edges than to the fold. Backstitch every few stitches to secure the stem to the background.

6. Roll the folded edge over the seam allowances. Appliqué the fold to the background fabric to create a smooth, thin stem.

Raw edges
Fold

Perfect Circles

I like to cut circular templates from heavy paper, such as a manila folder. You can also use heat-resistant template plastic. You will need a plastic circle stencil with circles in multiple sizes, available in art stores. Or, if you can find the correct sizes, paper punches used for scrapbooking projects will create perfectly round templates.

Note: You still need the plastic stencil to mark the fabric circles.

1. Place the circle stencil over the circle in your appliqué pattern to find the correct finished size for your design. Trace the circle onto heavy paper. Cut out the paper circle template, cutting as slowly and smoothly as possible. Use small, sharp scissors for best results.

2. Use the circle stencil again to trace onto your fabric a circle that is ½" larger in diameter than the paper circle. This adds a ¼"-wide seam allowance around the outer edge of the design. Cut out the fabric circle.

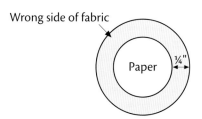

Wrong side of fabric

Paper

¼"

3. Using a small running stitch, sew within the seam allowance around the fabric circle, leaving at least 2" of thread at the beginning. Keep the stitches within the seam allowance, but not too close to the edge. Tie the two thread ends in a single knot and leave the thread ends loose.

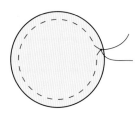

4. Place the paper template in the center of the fabric circle and pin them to your ironing board. Pull the thread ends to draw the seam allowance around the template.

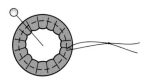

5. Steam press the fabric circle, using spray starch if you like, and then let the fabric cool for a minute. Carefully peel back the fabric and remove the paper circle. Gently pull the basting threads to tighten

the seam allowance again and make it lie flat. Tie another knot to secure the gathers, and trim the threads.

6. Pin the circle to the desired location on the background fabric and appliqué with smaller-than-usual stitches.

Dimensional Buds

1. Cut a 1½" square of fabric. Fold the square in half *diagonally*, wrong sides together.

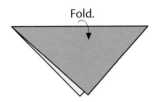

Fold.

2. Fold each side point down toward the bottom, overlapping the side points so they are about ¼" away from the bottom point. Baste along the bottom edges of the bud.

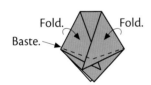

Fold.   Fold.

Baste.

3. Appliqué the calyx (base of the flower), leaving the top edge unstitched. Using tweezers, insert the bud into the calyx. Appliqué the top of the calyx, taking a few stitches all the way through to the background to secure the bud. The top fold of the bud isn't stitched to the background.

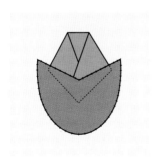

Gathered Blossoms

1. Cut a 2½"- to 3"-diameter circle from fabric. Lightweight cottons work well for these flowers.

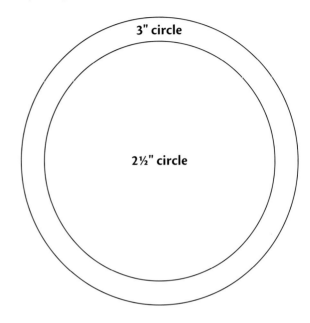

3" circle

2½" circle

2. Turn under ⅛" around the edge of the circle and sew a running stitch near the fold. Use a double thread about 18" long.

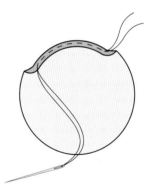

3. Gather the edges in to the center of the circle and tie a secure knot. If the edges don't meet tightly, take a few back-and-forth stitches at the center to close the hole.

4. Insert the needle straight down through the center of the gathers, bringing it through to the back (flat) side.

5. With the gathered side up, divide the circle into five equal sections as shown, marking lightly with a fabric marker.

6. To make the petals, bring the thread from the back over the outside edge of the flower (on the marked line) and insert it into the center again. Place the

thread at one of the edge markings, and then pull the thread to create a petal.

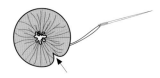

7. Continue looping the thread over the edges to make five petals. Knot the thread on the back of the flower but don't cut the thread. Add three beads to the flower center, and then tack the flower to the background fabric.

EMBROIDERY STITCHES

The following embroidery stitches are used throughout the book to add details to the projects.

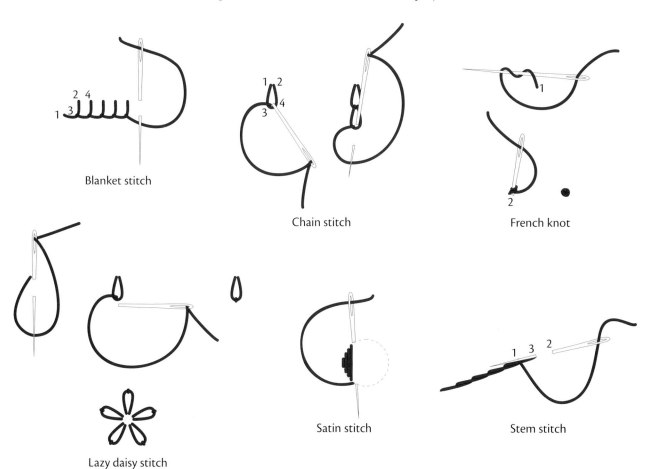

Blanket stitch

Chain stitch

French knot

Lazy daisy stitch

Satin stitch

Stem stitch

QUILT-TOP ASSEMBLY

From setting your blocks together to adding borders, you'll find details on assembling your quilt here.

Squaring up Blocks

Before you stitch your blocks together, it may be necessary to "square them up" to neaten the edges and make sure they're all the same size. Trim the edges using an acrylic ruler and rotary cutter. Be sure to leave ¼" seam allowance beyond any points or other important block details near the outside edges of your blocks.

If you've cut your appliqué blocks larger than necessary, trim them to the correct size. Use a large, square acrylic ruler or cut a piece of template plastic that is ½" larger (for ¼" seam allowances) than the finished block. Place the template plastic on the block, centering the design. Draw around the edges of the plastic, and then cut on the marked lines with scissors or a rotary cutter.

Straight Sets

In straight sets, blocks are laid out in horizontal rows that are parallel to the top and bottom edges of the quilt. Lay out the blocks on a flat surface. Sew the blocks together in rows; then join the rows to complete the patterned area of the quilt.

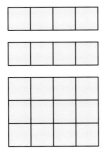

Diagonal Sets

Quilts that are set on point are constructed in diagonal rows, with setting triangles added around the edges to complete the corners and sides of the quilt. Lay out all the blocks and setting triangles on a flat surface before you start sewing. Make sure that all the blocks are the same size and absolutely square. Arrange the pieces in diagonal rows. Pick up and sew one row at a time; then join the rows to complete the quilt. Add the corner setting triangles last.

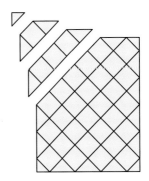

Borders

When the patchwork has been completed and the quilt blocks have been stitched together, borders add a finishing frame to your design. Some of the quilts in this book have borders with overlapped corners, while others have borders with mitered corners.

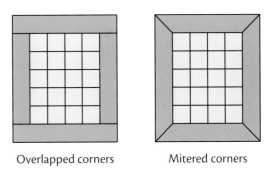

Overlapped corners   Mitered corners

Overlapped Corners

If you are making a large quilt or a quilt with many patchwork pieces, the size of the quilt can vary slightly from the stated size because of all the seams involved. For this reason, it's always a good idea to cut the borders to match your quilt. Check the size by measuring the quilt through the center of the patchwork. Sometimes the edges stretch, and a measurement of the center will be accurate and help you to avoid stretched and rippling borders. Cut the borders according to the center measurement of the quilt. Ease the edge of the quilt to fit the borders.

1. Attach the side borders to the quilt top first. Seam allowances may be pressed toward the border or toward the darker border when you're adding more than one border.

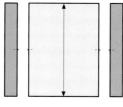

Measure center of quilt, top to bottom.

2. Stitch the top and bottom borders to the quilt top, overlapping the two side borders. Press the seam allowances in the same direction as the side borders.

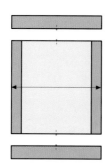

Measure center of quilt, side to side, including borders.

Mitered Corners

Estimate the finished outside dimensions of your quilt, including the width of the borders. Cut each border strip at least 1" longer than the required total length.

1. Fold each border strip in half crosswise and mark the center fold with a pin. Also, pin-mark the length of the quilt top on the border. Mark the center of each edge of the quilt top. Match the pins on the quilt top with the pins on the border strip. Pin the border strips to the quilt top.

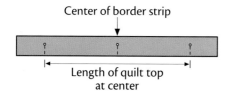

Center of border strip

Length of quilt top at center

2. Sew the border strips to the quilt top, beginning and ending ¼" from the raw edges of the quilt top. Press the seam allowances toward the border strips.

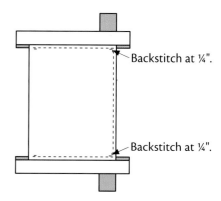

Backstitch at ¼".

Backstitch at ¼".

3. To miter a corner, lay the corner of the quilt top on a flat surface. Fold one border strip under so that the fold forms a 45° angle. Use a square ruler to check that the corner is flat and square. Press the fold to crease it.

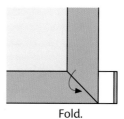

Fold.

4. Carefully center a piece of 1"-wide masking tape over the mitered fold. The tape will hold your miter in place while you sew the bias seam.

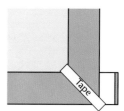

5. Open the mitered fold and use a pencil to draw a line on the crease.

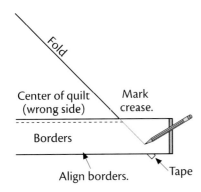

Center of quilt (wrong side)
Mark crease.
Borders
Align borders.
Tape

6. Stitch on the pencil line, through the two borders. Remove the tape.

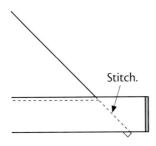

Stitch.

7. Make sure the seam lies flat on the quilt front and there are no pleats or puckers in the corner where the borders and quilt top meet. Cut away the excess fabric, leaving a ¼" seam allowance. Press the seam allowance open. Repeat for the remaining corners.

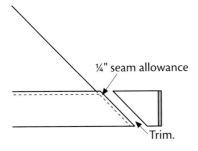

¼" seam allowance
Trim.

FINISHING TECHNIQUES

These days, many quilters use the services of professional long-arm machine quilters to have their projects quilted. If you choose that option, you will not need to mark the quilt top or layer and baste it. If you prefer to hand quilt your own project, use the instructions in this section for marking and hand quilting, as well as for adding binding to your quilt.

Marking the Quilting Designs

Quilting lines can follow the straight lines of patchwork in the quilt, outline the appliqué designs, or embellish spaces between the designs. It may not be necessary to mark the quilting designs if you are planning to quilt in the ditch (next to seams) or if you are outlining patchwork pieces.

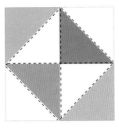 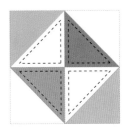

Quilt in the ditch   Outline quilt

Machine quilters often use free-motion designs that do not need to be marked on the fabric.

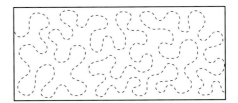

For other types of quilting, however, you'll probably want to mark the quilting designs. Do this before basting the three layers together. If the quilt lies flat during the marking process, lines will be smooth and accurate.

You can use a variety of tools to mark the quilting design onto the quilt top. You can use a regular pencil (#2 or #3), a fine-lead mechanical pencil, a silver marking pencil, or a chalk pencil or chalk marker for dark fabrics. A water-erasable marker can be used to mark the quilting design, but it may disappear before the quilting is completed if your weather is humid. Whichever tool you use for marking, test the tool on a sample of your fabric before using it on your quilt. Make sure you can see the lines, and make sure they can be removed.

To mark straight lines, use a long acrylic ruler. Parallel lines on acrylic rulers will help you keep the lines even. You can also use masking tape to mark straight lines. Simply quilt along the edge of the tape; then peel it off and your markings are removed.

To mark more elaborate quilting designs, place the quilt top on top of the quilting design and trace it onto the fabric. Use a light box if you have trouble seeing the design through the fabric. Another way to mark a design is to use a pre-cut plastic quilting stencil, readily available in quilt shops.

Hand Quilting

Before you begin to quilt, you must baste together the quilt top, batting, and backing. This secures the three layers and keeps the fabrics from slipping throughout the quilting process.

Hand quilting stitches are short running stitches used to sew the front, batting, and backing of your quilt together.

1. Thread a Between quilting needle with an 18" length of hand quilting thread and tie a single knot in the long end of the thread. Insert the needle through the top layer of the quilt about ¾" away from the point where you want to start stitching. Slide the needle through the batting layer and bring the needle out at the starting point.

2. Gently tug on the thread until the knot pops through the fabric and is buried in the batting. Take a backstitch and begin quilting, making a small running stitch that goes through all layers. Take two, three, or four stitches at a time, trying to keep them straight and even.

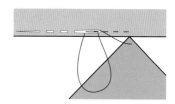

3. To end a line of quilting, make a single knot approximately ¼" from your quilt top. Take one more backstitch into your quilt, tugging the knot into the batting layer and bringing the needle out ¾" from your stitches. Clip the thread and let the end disappear into your quilt.

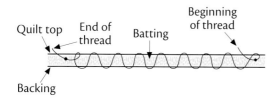

Binding

Binding adds the finishing touch to your quilt. It's a good idea to use dark fabrics to frame your design, although if you want your binding to blend in, you can use the same fabric as your outer border. Before attaching binding, machine-baste around the edge of the quilt to hold the layers together securely. Try to keep your stitches ⅛" from the edge of the quilt top. Trim any excess threads, batting, or backing even with the front cut edge of the quilt. Square up the corners of the quilt using a square acrylic ruler.

Measure the distance around the quilt and add 10". Cut and sew enough 2"-wide strips of binding fabric to equal this measurement.

Making Straight-Grain Binding

1. Cut 2"-wide strips across the width of the fabric using a rotary cutter and an acrylic ruler.

2. Sew the strips together, using diagonal seams, to create one long strip of binding. To make diagonal seams, cross two strip ends at right angles, right sides together. Lay these on a flat surface and imagine the strips as a large letter A. Draw a line across the crossed pieces to "cross the A," and then sew along the line. Your seam will be exact, and you can unfold a continuous strip.

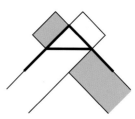 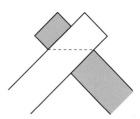

3. Trim the excess fabric, leaving a ¼"-wide seam allowance. Press this seam open to distribute the thickness of the seam.

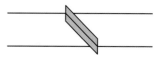

4. Fold the binding strip in half lengthwise, wrong sides together, and press with a hot steam iron.

Making Bias Binding

You must use bias binding for "Cottage Flowerpots" and "Yo-Yo Berries" because of the scalloped edges and for "Anniversary Roses" because of the curved corners.

To cut the bias binding, start with a single layer of fabric.

1. Cut bias strips by measuring an equal distance (6" or more) from a corner of your fabric. Place your ruler on these measurements and make a diagonal cut.

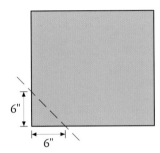

2. Align the bias-cut edge of the fabric with the 2" mark on your ruler and cut along the edge with your rotary cutter. Continue cutting 2"-wide strips until you have the number of strips necessary for the required binding length. After making several cuts, the fabric edge may be too long for your ruler. If this happens, carefully fold the fabric so the bias edges are even. Continue to cut the bias strips.

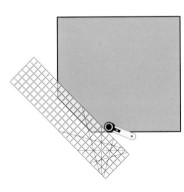

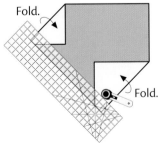

3. Sew the strips together and press them in half lengthwise as for straight-grain binding.

Applying Binding

1. Don't forget to square up the edges of the quilt and machine-baste around the quilt edges to securely hold the three layers together. Trim any excess threads, batting, or backing even with the front of the quilt.

2. Starting 6" from a corner, align the raw edges of the binding with the raw edges of the quilt. Start sewing 4" from the end of the binding using a ¼" seam allowance.

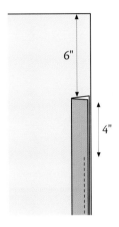

3. To miter the corners of the binding, stop stitching ¼" from the corner and backstitch.

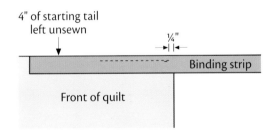

4. Fold the binding diagonally as shown on page 94, so that it extends straight up from the second edge of the quilt. Fold the binding back down so that it is even with the second edge of the quilt. The fold should be even with the first edge. Start sewing the

binding ¼" from the fold, making sure to backstitch. Repeat for the remaining corners.

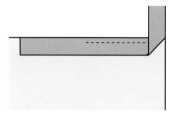

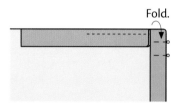

Fold.

5. To connect the ends of the binding, allow the end to overlap the beginning edge by 2". Open up the binding and cut the end diagonally so that the shortest end of the diagonal will be on top, nearest to you, when the binding is folded in half again. Turn the diagonal edge under ¼". Refold the binding and insert the beginning "tail" inside the diagonal fold. Continue sewing the binding onto the quilt.

Turn under ¼" on diagonal end.

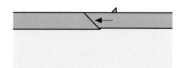

Tuck end inside.

6. Fold the binding over the edge of the quilt so it covers the stitching on the back of the quilt. When you fold the corners to the back of the quilt, a folded miter will appear on the front.

7. On the back, fold one side first and then the other to create a miter on the back.

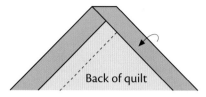

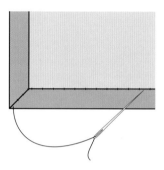

Back of quilt

8. Hand stitch the binding to the back of the quilt using the traditional appliqué stitch. I also hand stitch the corner folds and the diagonal connecting fold.

A Label for Your Quilt

You have made a very special quilt. Make a label for the back that includes your signature and the date. You will also want to include information about the quilt: a dedication, group-quilt information, or a story about your quilt.

Mimi Dietrich

Glorious Girl
2006

Writings of Mimi Dietrich

This bibliography is a complete record of my writings, and it includes the titles mentioned in this book. The titles are grouped so that you can see at a glance which ones are currently in print.

CURRENTLY IN PRINT

Happy Endings: Finishing the Edges of Your Quilt, Revised Edition. Woodinville, WA: Martingale & Company, 2003.

Easy Appliqué Samplers: 20 Designs to Mix and Match. Woodinville, WA: Martingale & Company, 2005.

Mimi Dietrich's Baltimore Basics: Album Quilts from Start to Finish. Woodinville, WA: Martingale & Company, 2006.

OUT OF PRINT

Happy Endings: Finishing the Edges of Your Quilt. Woodinville, WA: That Patchwork Place, 1987.

Handmade Quilts. Woodinville, WA: That Patchwork Place, 1990.

Baltimore Bouquets. Woodinville, WA: Martingale & Company, 1992.

The Easy Art of Appliqué: Techniques for Hand, Machine, and Fusible Appliqué. Woodinville, WA: That Patchwork Place, 1994.

Quilts from the Smithsonian: 12 Designs Inspired by the Textile Collection of the National Museum of American History. Woodinville, WA: That Patchwork Place, 1995

Quilts: An American Legacy. Woodinville, WA: That Patchwork Place, 1996.

Basic Quiltmaking Techniques for Borders and Bindings. Woodinville, WA: Martingale & Company, 1998.

Basic Quiltmaking Techniques for Hand Appliqué. Woodinville, WA: Martingale & Company, 1998.

Pink Ribbon Quilts: A Book Because of Breast Cancer. Woodinville, WA: Martingale & Company, 1999.

Bed and Breakfast Quilts: With Rise and Shine Recipes. Woodinville, WA: Martingale & Company, 2003.

Growing Up with Quilts: 15 Projects for Babies to Teens. Woodinville, WA: Martingale & Company, 2004.

About the Author

Mimi Dietrich lives in Baltimore, Maryland, and loves to appliqué. She has been writing books for That Patchwork Place (Martingale & Company) for 20 years. Her first book, *Happy Endings: Finishing the Edges of Your Quilt,* is an all-time bestseller that is still used by many quilters when they bind their quilts, and it has been expanded in a revised edition. Her favorite books are the ones with an appliqué theme, such as *Mimi Dietrich's Baltimore Basics* and *Easy Appliqué Samplers,* but Mimi has also written books with the Smithsonian Institution and a very special book of quilts for those whose lives have been touched by breast cancer. Now that Mimi has grandchildren, she has written a book of children's quilts with Sally Schneider, called *Growing Up with Quilts.* In 2006, Mimi designed a line of fabrics with P&B Textiles and the Baltimore Museum of Art based on her favorite Baltimore Album quilts. Visit Mimi's Web site at www.mimidietrich.com to see what she's working on next!

ACKNOWLEDGMENTS

Many, many thanks to:

Nancy Martin, who believed in me 20 years ago;

Everyone at Martingale & Company—you make my dreams come true!

Sharon Adams for making "Anniversary Roses";

Eleanor Eckman for making "Yo-Yo Berries";

Norma Campbell for inspiring "Cottage Flowerpots";

Karan Flanscha for sending me the "Mini Mimi" kit;

Linda Newsom and Laurie Gregg for your fabulous machine-quilting stitches;

Karen Brown for sharing your artist's energy;

Everyone at Seminole Sampler Quilt Shop for helping me with classes and fabric choices:
Barbara Blue, Arlene Chase, Jackie Clark, Alice Isenbart, Helen Quane, Robbyn Robinson, Libbie Rollman, Linda Schiffer, and Patty Stenpeck;

Kay Worley for the laughs;

Natalie Barnicle for the phone call;

Bob for your patience;

And Jon and Ryan—for living with quilts!